Also from Westphalia Press
westphaliapress.org

The Idea of the Digital University

Dialogue in the Roman-Greco World

The Politics of Impeachment

International or Local Ownership?:
Security Sector Development in
Post-Independent Kosovo

Policy Perspectives from Promising
New Scholars in Complexity

The Role of Theory in Policy Analysis

ABC of Criminology

Non-Profit Organizations and Disaster

The Idea of Neoliberalism: The
Emperor Has Threadbare
Contemporary Clothes

Donald J. Trump's Presidency:
International Perspectives

Ukraine vs. Russia: Revolution,
Democracy and War: Selected Articles
and Blogs, 2010-2016

Iran: Who Is Really In Charge?

Stamped: An Anti-Travel Novel

A Strategy for Implementing the
Reconciliation Process

Issues in Maritime Cyber Security

A Different Dimension: Reflections on
the History of Transpersonal Thought

Contracting, Logistics, Reverse
Logistics: The Project, Program and
Portfolio Approach

Unworkable Conservatism: Small
Government, Freemarkets, and
Impracticality

Springfield: The Novel

Lariats and Lassos

Ongoing Issues in Georgian Policy
and Public Administration

Growing Inequality: Bridging
Complex Systems, Population Health
and Health Disparities

Designing, Adapting, Strategizing in
Online Education

Secrets & Lies in the United Kingdom:
Analysis of Political Corruption

Pacific Hurtgen: The American Army
in Northern Luzon, 1945

Natural Gas as an Instrument of
Russian State Power

New Frontiers in Criminology

Feeding the Global South

Beijing Express: How to Understand
New China

Demand the Impossible: Essays in
History as Activism

Saber & Scroll

Volume 4
Issue 3
December 2015

Editor-in-Chief,
Joseph J. Cook

WESTPHALIA PRESS
An imprint of Policy Studies Organization

Saber & Scroll: Volume 4, Issue 3, December 2015
All Rights Reserved © 2019 by Policy Studies Organization

Westphalia Press
An imprint of Policy Studies Organization
1527 New Hampshire Ave., NW
Washington, D.C. 20036
info@ipsonet.org

ISBN-13: 978-1-63391-886-3
ISBN-10: 1-63391-886-6

Cover design by Jeffrey Barnes:
jbarnesbook.design

Daniel Gutierrez-Sandoval, Executive Director
PSO and Westphalia Press

Updated material and comments on this edition
can be found at the Westphalia Press website:
www.westphaliapress.org

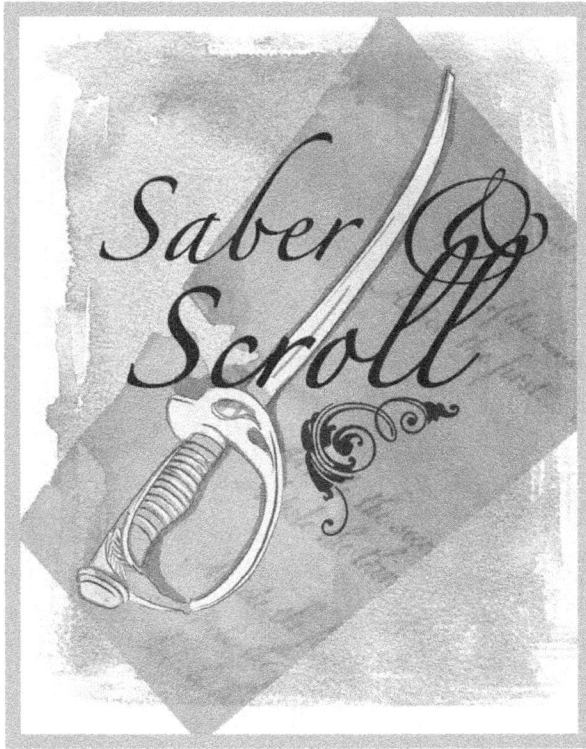

Saber and Scroll Journal

Volume IV Issue III

December 2015

Saber and Scroll Historical Society

Logo Design: Julian Maxwell

Cover Design: *Battle of Poitiers,* by Charles de Steuben, oil on canvas, c. 1834-1837.

Members of the Saber and Scroll Historical Society, the volunteer staff at the Saber and Scroll Journal publishes quarterly.

saberandscroll.weebly.com

Journal Staff

Editor-In-Chief
Joe Cook

Content Editors
Aida Dias, Mike Gottert, Rebecca Simmons Graf, Kathleen Guler,
Kyle Lockwood, Michael Majerczyk, Anne Midgley, Jack Morato,
and Chris Schloemer

Copy Editors
Michael Majerczyk, Anne Midgley

Proofreaders
Aida Dias, Frank Hoeflinger, Michael Majerczyk, Jack Morato, John
Persinger, Chris Schloemer, Robin Stewart, Susanne Watts

Webmaster
Jona Lunde

Academic Advisors
Emily Herff, Dr. Robert Smith, Jennifer Thompson

Contents

From the Editor   5

The Making of the Medieval papacy: the Gregorian Mission to Kent   7

Jack Morato

*Charles Martel turns South: The Hammer's campaigns in
Southern France 733-737*   35

Patrick S. Baker

*Benjamin Church, Joseph-François Hertel, and the Origins of Irregular
Warfare in the Early Colonial Period*   55

Christopher L. Hilmer

The Impact of Cars on Cities   69

Christopher N. Schloemer

The Zulu Identity: Surviving Colonialism, Apartheid, and King Shaka   83

Jessica R. Orr Flinchum

Huguenots and the French Enlightenment   95

Allison Ramsey

A Democratic Consideration of Herodotus's Histories   105

Mary Jo Davies

Book Reviews   115

Letter from the Editor

Welcome to the Fall 2015 issue of the *Saber and Scroll Journal*, produced by the American Public University System. This issue resulted from an open call for papers dealing with any topic in history or historiography. The result is a terrific collection of papers related to transformations in history: the birth of irregular warfare in colonial America, the changing face of city streets with the advent of automobiles, the evolving sense of Zulu identity, and others. In addition to these, we have compiled reviews of a wide-ranging group of books for your consideration.

This issue, itself, has been one of evolution. After a long and terrific run under Editor-In-Chief Anne Midgley, the *Journal* is now publishing its first issue with me as the new Editor-In-Chief. We have also seen turnover in our editorial team, and I am very encouraged by the fact that multiple people have expressed interest in joining our team, so we can all look forward to a bright future for our journal. I have to express special thanks to Anne for her close cooperation and help during this transitional issue. She has continued to tackle Microsoft Publisher and aid me in many of the other duties of the Editor-In-Chief. I look forward to hopefully giving her more of a rest in the production of our Winter 2016 issue, which has a call for papers presently open.

I wish to express gratitude to all of our editors for their hard work and to Dr. Robert Smith for his guidance. Back when I was an undergrad at Gettysburg College (before my graduate study at APUS), the school's motto was "Do Great Work." I believe we have truly done that with this issue. I also wish to extend thanks and gratitude to our authors—both those whose works appear in this issue, and those with whom we continue to work. The *Saber and Scroll Journal* is unique among academic journals; it would be difficult to find another journal where the editorial staff pays so much attention to every submission received. While many journals' calls for papers are essentially black holes for an author who does not hold a Ph.D., we at the *Saber and Scroll Journal* are committed to getting our authors' words into print—but at their highest possible quality. I will work hard to continue to do that for the rest of my term as your Editor-In-Chief.

Joseph J. Cook
Editor-In-Chief

The Making of the Medieval Papacy: The Gregorian Mission to Kent

Jack Morato

In the midst of the Western Roman Empire's collapse, Pope Leo I (r. 440-461) made the monumental assertion that the bishop of Rome was the true head of the Christian Church because Christ had designated Peter, Rome's first bishop, as the "foundation" of his earthly Church and the "doorkeeper" of his heavenly kingdom.[1] Leo's reasoning became known as the Petrine Doctrine, an idea that developed into the basis of papal power throughout the Middle Ages and the theological justification for papal hegemony over all bishops and patriarchs of Christendom—both in the Greek East and in the Latin West. In the mid-fifth century, however, the western portion of the Roman Empire had suffered an unrecoverable collapse, and Roman Christianity was supplanted in the provinces with either the pagan animism of the Anglo-Saxons and Franks or the heretical Arianism of the Goths and Vandals. Leo's bold proclamation of papal and Roman Catholic leadership did not coincide with social and political realities; he was writing at a time when the Roman Church held influence in Italy but little elsewhere. Establishing the authority of the Roman See in the Germanic kingdoms that occupied approximately what is now France, Spain, and Britain required the sustained efforts of successive popes and the churchmen who worked under their auspices. A key part of this long-range effort to translate the Petrine Doctrine from abstraction to reality included the late sixth-century mission to the Anglo-Saxon kingdom of Kent in Britain that Pope Gregory the Great (r. 590-604) organized. The Gregorian mission resulted in the conversion of the pagan Kentish kingdom and the establishment of the Episcopal Church at Canterbury, the first Latin Church in Britain since Roman times. More importantly, the Gregorian mission planted the seed of Latin Christianity in Britain and culminated in the conversion of the whole island less than a century later under the leadership of the pope in Rome.

Pope Leo and Pope Gregory were visionaries who foresaw a universal church that would bring Latin Christianity to the new Germanic kingdoms of Western Europe. In the late sixth century, however, their vision was exactly that and nothing more. The prestige and authority of the Latin Church can be counted among the victims of the Germanic invasions of the fifth century. That the Latin Church was still extant in Gregory's time was no small miracle in itself.

Throughout late antiquity and the early Middle Ages the Church had no army of its own to enforce its will or guard its interests; it was dependent upon secular authority for protection, the suppression of heresy, and the granting of economic and legal concessions.

The years between 400 and 600 were a transitory period for the Church, even more so perhaps than for Western European society in general. It was a time of tremendous flux in church-state relations that saw the Church in search of secular authorities stable and powerful enough to nurture its interests and protect it from those who would do it harm both physically and spiritually. The Roman Empire had filled this role during the last years of its existence. Emperor Constantine's conversion in the early fourth century inaugurated the remarkable transformation of Christianity from a persecuted, underground religion of beggars to the state-sanctioned religion of the Caesars.[2] Theodosius I (r. 379-395), the last emperor of any great consequence, vigorously proscribed both Roman paganism and Arian Christianity—the most important spiritual rivals of Latin Christianity. To these gifts were added a number of fiscal and judicial privileges that allowed the Church to develop the independence it later relied upon to withstand the Roman collapse. Members of the clergy were granted substantial tax exemptions, and the Church was allowed to develop its own canon law and hold its own tribunals that effectively meant the Roman state surrendered jurisdiction over members of the clergy.[3] The emperors of the Christian Roman Empire thus ensured the continuity of the nascent Church, and at the end of the Roman era the Latin Church found itself in the unenviable position of being the only institution capable of ameliorating the unsettled society of post-invasion Europe.

The disordered condition of early medieval Europe prevented the popes from exercising any real leadership in the two hundred years following the Roman collapse. Indeed, Leo and Gregory were two anomalies in an otherwise steady decline in papal influence. Most of the fifth and sixth century popes did nothing to advance Pope Leo's grand vision of papal authority and ecclesiastical leadership. Survival, preservation, and adjustment occupied the intellectual energies of churchmen during this tumultuous period.

Pope Gregory came to the papal throne in the late sixth century at the nadir of papal and Church influence. Gregory was painfully aware of the desperate condition of the Church and the monumental task that stood before him. In a pessimistic letter written shortly after his accession, Gregory compared the Church to an "old and grievously shattered ship," constantly taking on water and "battered by a daily and violent storm."[4]

With enemies threatening on all sides, the position of the pope in Italy was precarious at best. The Ostrogoths and their leader Theodoric were defeated during the Gothic War (535-554) and replaced by the Byzantines who, under the direction of Emperor Justinian I (r. 527-565), had sought to reclaim their "authority over the remaining countries which the ancient Romans possessed . . . [and were] . . . lost by subsequent neglect."[5] Byzantine rule did not last in Italy, its power weakened with the invasion of the Lombards, a particularly barbaric tribe of Germans who invaded northern Italy in 568. The Lombards in Gregory's day held the whole of Cisalpine Gaul up to the Alpine passes through which Hannibal had trekked some eight hundred years before. They also held Beneventum, Spoletum, and parts of Tuscany in the south. The Byzantines meanwhile retained Ravenna, Istria, Venetia, and Naples in addition to the islands of Sardinia, Corsica, and Sicily. As pope, Gregory maintained possession of the *Patrimonium Sancti Petri* consisting mainly of lands in the vicinity of Rome, Dalmatia, southern Gaul, and Sicily.

The violence and instability of his surroundings distressed Gregory. He spoke of the terrible "suffering from the swords of the Lombards in the daily plundering and mangling and slaying of our citizens"[6] and complained of the danger he faced and the "confusion of the tribulations which we suffer in this land."[7] Unlike his ineffectual predecessors, however, Gregory was not one to sit idle. The pope worked through the Christian Lombard Queen Theodelinda to soften the behavior of the Lombards.[8] His efforts eventually paid off. Theodelinda's son Adaloaldus was baptized a Christian and succeeded his father as king in 616.[9] The Byzantines retained control of North Africa and substantial portions of Italy, but no harmony developed between Rome and Constantinople. The caesaro-papist ideology of the Byzantine emperors meant that both the pope and the Byzantine emperor competed for absolute supremacy in ecclesiastical affairs. Gregory was cordial towards the Byzantine emperor, but in doing so, his aim was not conciliation but placation. The pope was simply buying time while he carried out his important work in Western Europe.

Most of Western Europe had fallen away from the Latin Church. The Visigoths controlled the Iberian Peninsula—what is now Spain and Portugal. They were a primitive tribe that had been among the first to invade Roman territory. They initially subscribed to Arian Christianity, a heretical interpretation of the nature of Christ that orthodox Christians condemned. The Arian heresy had spread virulently throughout the eastern provinces of the Roman Empire before Theodosius's vigorous persecutions crushed it in 383 and 384. Official persecution, however, came too late to prevent the spread of Arianism beyond the Danube frontier where it contaminated the Goths shortly before their romp through Roman Gaul and Hispania.[10] King Reccared I (r. 586-601) of the Visigoths converted in 587 "from the error of Arian heresy to the firmness of a right faith"—that is, Latin

Christianity—shortly before Gregory assumed the Throne of Peter.[11] The conversion of the Visigoths was a cause to celebrate, but it did little for the Latin Church for two reasons. First, the Visigothic kings were singularly inept in the arts of government and administration. The orthodox Spanish population detested them for this reason and because the kings clung to tribal Arianism for two hundred years after arriving in Spain. The Visigoths, through their incompetence and their alien faith, failed to win the loyalty of the locals. Deprived of support, the Visigothic kingdom eventually succumbed to the Moslem invasion of Iberia in the early eighth century. Second, there is not enough evidence to suggest that Gregory was able to exert any influence over the direction of the Spanish Church or the conduct of the Visigothic kings. Gregory's letter to Reccared drips of adulation and sermon, and it clearly shows the pontiff's intent on Christianizing that kingdom and ameliorating the savage behavior of its kings.[12] Gregory also dispatched a letter to a man named Claudius who appears to have been influential in the court of the Gothic king, but the correspondence is vague and refers neither to the good deeds that provoked Gregory's praise nor to the precise station of Claudius.[13] These two dispatches represent the extent of Gregory's activism in Spain.

The religious situation in Merovingian France was more optimistic, but even there the condition of the Church was feeble at best. The Salian Franks came into Gaul as pagans, but they converted to Latin Christianity during the reign of Clovis I (r. 481-509). Though Gregory of Tours lauded Clovis as "another Constantine,"[14] the conversion of the Franks ultimately did little to restore papal influence in Gaul. The Franks, like their Germanic cousins elsewhere in Europe, were a primitive and violent people who came to Gaul with unsophisticated legal and political systems and almost no concept of statehood. They possessed a deep-seated hatred for Roman civilization. The political organization of the Germanic tribes at the time of the Roman collapse centered on the war-band, what the medieval historian Norman Cantor called an "irresponsible type of kingship resting . . . upon military prestige."[15] War chiefs exercised societal leadership by commanding what was essentially an armed gang. Loyalty rested on the leader's ability to provide opportunities for plunder. Religious conversion could not dilute the primitivism of the Frankish rulers, and the sixth-century Merovingian kings quite literally ran their country into the ground. They did nothing to ameliorate society, and they spent their energies satisfying their base desires and fighting over the throne. The Frankish contempt of Roman institutions meant that they preserved nothing of the Roman administrative structure. As in Spain, the ineptitude of the royal house caused the locals to hate them. Political and economic power began to decentralize in the early sixth century as the Gallo-Roman and Frankish nobility began carving up large, hereditary estates for themselves at the expense of the Merovingian royal family.[16] Preoccupied with their infighting, the ruling house did nothing to stop this process.

The bishops of Gaul initially placed a tremendous amount of faith in their alliance with the Merovingian royal house. They thought it possible to resurrect that happy congruence of secular and ecclesiastical authority that had proved so beneficial to the Church during the last century of Roman rule. Frankish barbarism precluded such a union, and the Gallic churchmen soon turned away from the Merovingian kings in disgust. Their disappointment is reflected in the unmistakable narrowing of vision among the higher clergy. Deprived of a conscientious secular authority that could bring about a Christian society, the French bishops resigned themselves to building up their own private estates in the manner of the secular Frankish nobility.[17] The bishop and historian Gregory of Tours's *History of the Franks* is representative of the disillusionment and pessimism of the late sixth century French bishops. The work is peppered with disgust at the destructive behavior of the Merovingian kings and the generally savage conditions that prevailed.[18]

The situation in Spain, Gaul, and Italy imparted a dreary backdrop to Pope Gregory's chosen task of establishing papal authority throughout Western Europe. The pope's leaky ship was in need of repair, and he chose Britain as a starting point. The situation in Britain had been perhaps bleakest of all. Christianity had arrived in Britain some two centuries before the Roman collapse,[19] but the coming of the Anglo-Saxons in the mid-fifth century dealt a serious blow to the faith. The Angles, Jutes, and Saxons who arrived in Britain were almost entirely untouched by Roman civilization,[20] and like the other Germanic tribes who came across the frontier, their socio-political and legal systems were rudimentary at best. They were ruled by a warrior chieftain whose hold on power depended upon the size of his army and his abilities as a warrior.[21] No aristocracy or nobility existed to speak of; most people belonged to a large class of free peasant farmers.[22] The Anglo-Saxons were illiterate, and they harbored a special hatred of urban life. They held few qualms over burning libraries, levelling what remained of the Roman cities, and enslaving the Romano-Celtic inhabitants. "Peace," according to Tacitus, "is repulsive to the race."[23] The late British historian Jasper Ridley agreed, calling them "the most destructive immigrants who have ever come to Britain."[24] The native Britons were poor fighters, and their inability to unite amongst themselves meant that they could not match the aggression of the Germanic invaders.[25] The regions that now approximate Scotland, Wales, and Cornwall were all that remained of British territory by the end of the sixth century. Elmet, Rheged, Gododdin, and several other smaller British kingdoms to the west and north of Northumbria fared better than their southern counterparts, but they soon lost their independence to Anglo-Saxon expansionism throughout the seventh century.[26]

The process of conquest spurred changes in Anglo-Saxon society. A more stable form of semi-hereditary kingship developed in which a male of the royal line succeeded the king. An armed retinue of warrior nobles drawn from prominent families attended the king. By the time Gregory's missionaries arrived in 597,[27] Britain south of the River Tyne was a pagan land comprised of more than a dozen independent kingdoms, each governed by its own royal house. The overriding objective of these kingdoms from their formation beginning in the mid-fifth century was to acquire and maintain power at the expense of their neighbors.[28] The result was a period of unabated internecine warfare five centuries long. Nothing, not even the arrival of Christianity, could temper Anglo-Saxon destructiveness.[29]

The British Isles were not devoid of Christianity when Gregory's mission arrived in Kent under the leadership of his chosen emissary, the Benedictine monk Augustine. It persisted in Ireland, an island so wild that the Romans had never tried to conquer it, yet it became the great preserver of the Christian tradition in the British Isles. Irish monks meticulously copied and preserved great libraries of classical works in their dimly lit monasteries.[30] From these bases at the edge of the world, the sixth-century Irish monks set about converting the Scots, Picts, and English who resided in the wild territories of northern Britain.

Christianity had first come to Ireland in the fifth century through Patricius, a Roman Briton known today as Saint Patrick, the Apostle of Ireland. Abducted at the age of sixteen by Irish raiders, Patrick spent six miserable years as the slave of a pagan Irish chieftain.[31] The traumatic experience of incessant hunger and exposure had a profound effect on him. Like many in such desperate circumstances, he turned to God and developed an intense spirituality and sense of mission.[32] Patrick escaped and eventually found his way back to Britain, but he could not sit still knowing that the Irish remained pagans. He returned and worked tirelessly to convert his former captors until most Irish were Christians by the time of his death around the middle of the fifth century.[33] From the beginning, the rough nature of Ireland's apostle set Irish Christianity on an independent course. Patrick spent his entire life at the periphery of civilization and, unlike his counterparts elsewhere in the Romanized world, he was not a scholar. His education was cut short by his abduction,[34] a fact revealed in his simplistic use of Latin rife with grammatical errors.[35] Patrick's isolated upbringing, coupled with his deficient classical education, ensured the Christianity he brought to the Irish was unencumbered by the legacy of the Greco-Roman world.

Ireland was an illiterate country devoid of urbanization when Patrick arrived, a veritable tabula rasa. While the early Church had emerged within the Roman state and was shaped by it, the reverse held in Ireland. Unlike elsewhere in the Roman world, there was no preexisting infrastructure in Ireland—either political or physical—for Christianity to graft itself upon when it arrived in the fifth century. Therefore, Christianity helped to shape Irish civilization to a much greater extent than in the rest of the former Roman Empire. As the first monks formed monastic communities dedicated to learning and the preservation of classical texts, their religious houses drew thousands of students and converts hoping to benefit from what the monks had to offer. Unsurprisingly, the nuclei of Ireland's first urban centers sprang from the monastic repositories of classical learning and holy wisdom.

Ireland's isolation shielded it from the tumult unfolding in Britain and gave its Christianity time to crystallize. From their sanctuary at the fringe of civilization, Irish monks spread further afield into Scotland, northern Britain, and continental Europe. Some one hundred years after Patrick's death, Irish missionaries under the leadership of the unstoppable monk Columba (521-597) arrived in Pictland (Scotland) and succeeded in converting both the Scots and the northern Picts.[36] Columba founded the religious community on the island of Iona in 564, a place that soon became an important center of learning and piety. Columba, along with his intrepid brothers from Iona, then went on to found dozens of monasteries throughout

Figure 1 *Saint Columba in Pictland*, by J. R. Skelton in Henrietta Elizabeth Marshall, *Scotland's Story*, 1906.

Scotland.[37] Iona became an important base for new missions into Pictland and northern England, and it became a nexus of Celtic Christianity for the next two centuries. Irish monks from Iona were also active in the powerful Northumbrian kingdom in the early seventh century.[38] Among them was Aidan, an Irish monk known as the Apostle of Northumbria for his spectacular success there under the patronage of the Bernician king Oswald (604-641).[39] Significantly, Aidan, an Irishman, was Northumbria's first bishop. He established his see on the island of Lindisfarne, a place that would later play an important role in ecclesiastical history.[40]

The intellectual and missionary work of the Irish monks would have ordinarily been encouraging for Gregory. However, Celtic Christianity— sometimes called Insular Christianity—differed in a number of ways from the Latin Christianity of the Roman Church. These differences were largely superficial, for both Latin and Celtic Christians agreed on all the major theological points.[41] Still, the peculiar habits of the Insular Christians troubled orthodox adherents of the Roman Church. The ecclesiastical organization of the Celtic Church was unique in that the monastery and not the cathedral dominated the ecclesiastical landscape, and abbots, not bishops, exercised authority.[42] Indeed, there were no dioceses and diocesan clergy at all.[43] Bishops had been sources of stability and leadership since the Roman era, and for many Latin churchmen a hierarchy without bishops was both untenable and unholy.[44] The nature of Insular monasticism was unique as well, based on the loose cenobitic type more commonly found in the eastern Mediterranean in which the abbot enjoyed only a loose control over the individual brothers. Insular monks were also known for their singular knowledge of Greek and their possession of a number of important Greek texts, most of which could not be found anywhere else in early medieval Europe.[45]

The two most important points of divergence, judging from their frequent mentions in the *Historia Ecclesiastica Gentis Anglorum (Ecclesiatical History of the English People)* written in the eighth century by the Northumbrian monk Bede (c. 672-735), were the shape of the tonsure and the reckoning of the date of Easter. Celtic churchmen *looked* different from their Latin counterparts, and this reinforced their "otherness" in the eyes of the Roman churchmen who took issue with it ostensibly because of its association with the biblical heretic Simon Magus.[46] The more important dispute was the different calculation for the date of Easter.[47] Despite incessant appeals from Roman churchmen, Insular Christians persisted in their Celtic interpretation of Easter for over a century after Latin Christianity took hold in Kent.[48]

If the unorthodox practices of Insular Christians were not enough to concern Gregory, the swaggering behavior of the missionary Columbanus (543-615) certainly was. Columbanus was a rough Irish monk with a profound sense of duty much like Saint Columba before him. Columbanus became Irish Christianity's continental representative, making it his mission to proselytize to the pagans of Europe. His chosen theatre was Gaul, to which he went around 590 to establish as many monastic communities as he could. Columbanus was very successful; his monasteries in Gaul and Lombardy attracted many new adherents to the faith. Soon, however, the Latin bishops of Gaul took issue with his activities within their jurisdiction. The Gallic bishops were a proud and petty lot, much more interested in building up their worldly estates than spreading the Gospel. These men never left the comfort of their dioceses, unwilling to subject themselves to worldly hardships for the sake of preaching to the Frankish masses. The bishops summoned Columbanus to a synod, presumably to assert their authority over him and to correct his erroneous interpretation of Easter, but Columbanus had no intention of appearing before them. Instead, he sent a defiant letter in which he castigated the bishops for their myopic worldliness and lectured them in the virtues of pious humility and clerical poverty.[49]

Intending to plead the case for the Celtic date of Easter, Columbanus wrote to Pope Gregory around the time of his quarrel with the Gallic bishops. His letter was couched in respectful pleasantries, but it clearly revealed that Columbanus had no intention of submitting to the Pope's authority. He addressed Gregory not as the supreme head of Christendom but as a colleague, urging him to accept the Insular interpretation of Easter. Further, Columbanus prodded the pope to correct the erroneous interpretations of his predecessors and poked fun at Pope Leo's name in the process. "Better by far is a living dog," wrote Columbanus, "in this problem than a dead lion."[50] Gregory's response is not extant. The pope may have opted for pontifical silence in the face of such insolence, or his reply may have been lost in transit. The source of Columbanus's boldness is also difficult to ascertain. Perhaps it was, as scholar Thomas Cahill asserted, a consequence of his "Irishness," his innate playfulness, and honesty.[51] More likely, however, the secular behavior of the Gallic bishops disgusted Columbanus. In any event, Columbanus's rebellious tone could have only heightened Gregory's fear of losing control of Britain to the Irish monks who were spreading in all directions from their monasteries in Scotland.

His alarm over an impending rift between the two churches aside, Gregory may have been genuinely concerned for the souls of the pagan English. This hypothesis is derived from the well-known tale in Bede's *Historia* of Gregory's encounter with some Deiran slave children. According to Bede,

He inquired whether those islanders were Christians, or still involved in the errors of paganism, and was informed that they were pagans. Then fetching a deep sigh from the bottom of his heart, "Alas! what pity," said he, "that the author of darkness should own men of such fair countenances; and that with such grace of outward form, their minds should be void of inward grace." He therefore again asked, what was the name of that nation? and was answered, that they were called Angles. "Right," said he, "for they have an angelic face, and it is meet that such should be co-heirs with the Angels in heaven.[52]

The episode, which had occurred before Gregory attained the Throne of Peter, made the pontiff aware of English paganism, and spurred his resolve to bring Christianity to Britain. Evidence suggests that Gregory never forgot those English children he met at the Roman marketplace. In 595, after he became pope, Gregory directed his agent Candidus to use some of the proceeds of the papal estates in

Figure 2 *St. Gregory before his Elevation to the Royal Chair observing some Children of Great Beauty set up for Sale in the Slave Market at Rome,* Painted by Heny Singleton, engraved by Piercy Roberts, 1801.

Gaul to purchase English slaves there so they could be sent to a monastery for their salvation.[53]

Whether motivated by genuine compassion, power, or both, Gregory understood that he needed to act quickly lest the Irish monks succeed at converting the Anglo-Saxons to their unorthodox version of Christianity. Between the Roman and Irish monks sat pagan England, a prize waiting for whoever could get to the pagan kings first. One of Gregory's few flaws was his small-minded perspective towards the Celtic monks. Like his contemporaries, he perceived them as rivals instead of allies and the conversion of England as a contest between Rome and Iona. A race for the souls of the English began as soon as Augustine landed in Kent.

Gregory took decisive action, marshaling all the resources at his disposal to ensure the success of his missionaries. He dispatched Augustine together with a small band of forty Benedictine monks in 596 to that "barbarous, fierce, and unbelieving nation" of Kent in southeast Britain.[54] The pope's many letters to Augustine and others reveal that he was personally invested in the direction of the mission and its outcome. Gregory sent letters urging the bishops and nobility of Gaul, the territory through which Augustine and his brethren needed to travel on their way to Kent, urging them to grant the monks safe passage and whatever assistance they could give.[55] Gregory's entreaties paid off; the Frankish king and clergy welcomed the mission.[56] The Benedictine monks landed on the Isle of Thanet in the following year and immediately made contact with the Kentish ruler Ethelbert. The king ordered them to remain where they were and supplied them with necessities while he decided what to do with them.[57] Ethelbert soon visited, and Augustine seized the opportunity to preach the "word of life" to him.[58] The king was swayed but did not convert immediately. He did, however, give the monks permission to evangelize in his kingdom and allowed them to settle in Canterbury, the main town in Kent.[59] The monks began practicing their simple way of life according to the Rule of Benedict, attracting numerous converts.[60] King Ethelbert was baptized soon after, prompting the Kentish nobility and a large proportion of the population to convert as well.[61] Bede mentioned that the king did not compel his subjects to convert but that they did so out of their own free will.[62] In a jubilant letter dated 597 to Eulogius, the Bishop of Alexandria, Gregory informed him of the conversion of ten thousand English.[63] Gregory made Augustine "archbishop of the English nation" in that same year.[64]

Interestingly, the pagan authorities of Kent received Gregory's missionaries better than the British churchmen did. Augustine's early interactions with Celtic churchmen established in southern Britain reinforced Gregory's suspicions of an inevitable schism. The initial meeting between the Latin monks and the Celtic churchmen was unproductive and peppered with animosity. The Insular monks proved uncooperative and unwilling to preserve "the unity of the church," according to Bede.[65] They "preferred their own traditions" and "could not depart from their ancient customs," namely, the Celtic date of Easter.[66] Moreover, Augustine's inflated perception of his own importance as the representative of the one universal Church caused him to be tactless and arrogant. He failed to rise from his seat at the Celts' approach, angering them and convincing them that one so pompous could not possibly be the bearer of God's truth.[67] Failing to reason with them, Augustine subsequently threatened them with divine vengeance, which, predictably, had little effect.[68]

The rivalry between the Insular and Roman Churches is prominently displayed in Bede's *Historia Ecclesiastica*. Bede was an Englishman who spent his entire life working in the Northumbrian monastery at Jarrow, a Latin religious house. To a degree, the purpose of his *Historia* was to highlight God's workings in the world, and in this way it conformed to the eschatological and linear concept of history prevalent in Christianity since apostolic times. Significantly, however, Bede sought to emphasize the victory of *Latin Christianity* in Britain and the achievements of Anglo-Saxon Church unity under the leadership of Canterbury—the first and most important Latin Church in Britain. This bias affected his treatment of events. For example, he downplayed the interactions between the Northumbrian and Celtic kingdoms and overstated Northumbrian interactions with the English kingdoms to the south.[69] He also discounted the contributions of the Irish monks in the conversion of England.[70]

Bede's coverage of the early seventh-century conflict between the Anglo-Saxon kings Penda of Mercia and Edwin of Deira is a case in point. Edwin converted to Latin Christianity in 627, and his baptism by the Roman monk Paulinus prompted mass conversions of the Northumbrian people.[71] Penda, the pagan king of the aggressive Mercian kingdom in central England, entered into an alliance of convenience with the Welsh prince Cadwallon of Gwynedd, a Celtic Christian. Together, the two defeated and killed Edwin, then proceeded to massacre the newly-baptized inhabitants of Northumbria. Predictably, this inaugurated a period of apostasy as converts renounced their new faith to avoid persecution.[72] Though both Penda and Cadwallon shared guilt for their atrocities, Bede's ireful pen lashed Cadwallon the hardest:

> [O]ne of the chiefs, by whom it was carried on, was a pagan, and
> the other a barbarian, more cruel than a pagan; for Penda, with all
> the nation of the Mercians, was an idolater, and a stranger to the

name of Christ; but Caedwalla, though he professed and called himself a Christian, was so barbarous in his disposition and manner of living.[73]

Cadwallon—that "unrighteous instrument of rightful vengeance," as Bede called him[74]—was cast as the ultimate villain, a Christian who had betrayed his brothers in Christ by siding with the pagan warlord Penda. The fact that Cadwallon was a Celtic Christian only served Bede's purpose in casting Celtic Christianity as inferior to Latin Christianity.

Bede's hostility to Celtic Christianity is also displayed in his coverage of the earlier slaughter of British monks at Chester in 616. Ethelfrith, the Bernician king of Northumbria, embarked on a punitive expedition to Wales to enforce his overlordship there. When he arrived at Chester, he found approximately two thousand Celtic monks from the monastery at Bangor gathered in prayer against him. They chanted prayers and sang psalms for the victory of the Welsh. Ethelfrith slaughtered almost twelve hundred of them along with the entire Welsh army. Bede's mention of this failure of Christian prayer highlights that the monks were Celtic rather than Latin Christians. Their death at the hands of a pagan lord was punishment for their earlier failure to submit to the direction of Augustine and the Roman Church.[75] Bede also addressed the animosity between the Celtic and Latin churchmen directly, noting that even in his own day, some 130 years after the arrival of Roman Christianity, it was "the custom of the Britons to despise the faith and religion of the English, and to have no part with them in anything any more than with pagans."[76]

Gregory continued to communicate with his missionaries long after their arrival in Kent. Through frequent correspondences, he directed their efforts, provided encouragement, and answered questions. Gregory sent a shipment of supplies to Augustine in 601 consisting of "vessels and altar-cloths . . . church furniture, and vestments for the bishops and clerks."[77] He also sent instructions for the episcopal organization of Britain. Telling of his great insight, moderation, and practical wisdom, Gregory directed Augustine to be flexible in administering his see. Gregory understood that the English church was in its infancy and that strict adherence to the minutia of orthodoxy might be counterproductive.[78] Gregory's sensibility and practicality was also on display in his softening of the harsh Augustinian (of Hippo) stance on the nature of free will and salvation. The early Christian theologian and philosopher St. Augustine (354-430) taught that salvation was a consequence of divine grace and that humans could do nothing to earn that grace. This stance would have severely hindered the early medieval church's effort to convert the pagan masses: if good works did nothing to assure salvation, people would have no incentive to act in accordance with God's will. The ultimate evangelist, Gregory, took a much more moderate approach. He posited that individuals did not need to worry about salvation as long as they received the sacraments and lived according to the moral teachings of the Church. This was in violation of St. Augustine of Hippo's position but necessary if the Church was to be successful at converting the Germanic masses.

The conversion of Kent was only the beginning. Gregory praised King Ethelbert for his piety, but he also urged him to "make haste to extend the Christian faith among the peoples under thy sway [and] redouble the zeal of thy rectitude in their conversion. . . . make haste to infuse into the kings and peoples subject to you the knowledge of God." The pope implored the Kentish king to "build up the manners of thy subjects in great purity of life by exhorting, by terrifying, by enticing, by correcting, by shewing examples of well-doing."[79] Gregory clearly had grand designs for his new Constantine in Britain, and Ethelbert did not disappoint. The Kentish king set about bringing Christianity to those kingdoms over which he enjoyed influence. King Sabert of Essex converted in 604 due to Ethelbert's intervention. Ethelbert also built and endowed the original St. Paul's Church in London according to Gregory's plan.[80] Further, Ethelbert attempted to convert the East Anglian king Raedwald. Though Raedwald refused and died a pagan, he did erect a Christian altar in his kingdom.[81] The kingdoms of Mercia and Wessex were slower to accept Christianity owing to their independence from Kentish influence. King Penda of Mercia clung stubbornly to paganism, but he later allowed his son and daughter to marry the Christian children of the Bernician royal house for political purposes. Penda's children turned Mercia into a Christian kingdom after his death in the Battle of the River Winwaed in 654.[82] Christianity took hold slowest in Wessex. A Frankish bishop named Birinus came to Wessex with the sanction of Pope Honorius I to preach there, and he was successful at winning the conversion of the first West Saxon ruler Cynegils in 635.[83] Cynegils's son and successor Coinwalch refused to convert initially, but he did later due to the influence of King Anna of the East Angles in whose court he spent a period of exile.[84]

The ecclesiastical history of Northumbria (comprised of Bernicia and Deira in the early seventh century) is second in importance only to that of Kent, as the kings of Northumbria ultimately chose to side with the Latin churchmen of Canterbury at the Synod of Whitby in 664. Latin Christianity came to Northumbria through the conversion of Edwin of Deira (r. 616-633). In 604, the pagan king of Bernicia, Ethelfrith, invaded Deira and slew the Deiran king Ethelric, prompting

Edwin, Ethelric's kinsman, to flee for his life. Edwin spent many years in exile among the southern English where he was drawn into the orbit of Latin Christianity. In 625, Edwin married Ethelbert's daughter, the Christian Kentish princess Ethelburh. Edwin did not immediately convert, but a condition of the marriage contract required Edwin to provide tolerance of Christians within his kingdom.[85] A Roman monk from Canterbury named Paulinus accompanied Ethelburh to Northumbria, ostensibly to serve as her holy advisor. In reality, however, Paulinus dreamed of converting the Northumbrian king and his people.[86] In this effort, Pope Boniface V assisted Paulinus. The pope sent a letter to King Edwin, urging him to accept Christianity without further delay. He also corresponded with Queen Ethelburh, imploring her to persuade her husband to convert.[87] These efforts eventually bore fruit, and Edwin was baptized by Paulinus on Easter in 627.[88]

The conversion of Northumbria was consistent with the typical modus operandi of the Church in its efforts to convert the Germanic rulers of Western Europe. The Church found it easier to convert the queen of a pagan ruler, then recruit her help in converting her husband. The letter Pope Boniface V wrote to Edwin's queen Ethelburh, reflected this method:

> Persist, therefore, illustrious daughter, and to the utmost of your power endeavour to soften the hardness of his heart by carefully making known to him the Divine precepts; pouring into his mind a knowledge of the greatness of that mystery which you have received by faith, and of the marvellous reward which, by the new birth, you have been made worthy to obtain…Strive, both in season and out of season, that with the co-operating power of our Lord and Saviour Jesus Christ, your husband also may be added to the number of Christians.[89]

Bertha, the Merovingian Christian queen of Ethelbert, received a similar letter from Pope Gregory in which he urged her to "strengthen by continual hortation the mind of your glorious husband in love of the Christian faith; let your solicitude infuse into him increase of love for God."[90] The technique is also revealed in Gregory's letters to the Christian Lombard queen Theodelinda.[91] Paul the Deacon in his *Historia Langobardorum* claimed that the Lombard king Agilulf's wife persuaded him to accept Christianity.[92] Even the Christian queen Clotilda persuaded her husband, Clovis I, the first Christian king of the Franks, to abandon his paganism.[93] The church leveraged the influence wives had, and continued to have, over their husbands.

As mentioned previously, King Edwin of Diera in Northumbria was later defeated and killed in a conflict with Penda and Cadwallon. This prompted Northumbria to enter a period of apostasy due to abuses the victors inflicted on Christians. Christianity was restored under Oswald (r. 634-642), a son of Ethelfrith of Bernicia who, unlike his father, was a devout Christian. Bede called Oswald "the most Christian king" for his role in reintroducing Christianity to the Northumbrian kingdom and establishing the important religious center at Lindisfarne.[94] Oswald differed from his predecessor in two ways. Coming from the Bernician royal house, he was heavily exposed to Insular Christianity. While Edwin had fled south, Oswald and his brother Oswiu fled to Ireland and Scotland where they were introduced to Celtic Christianity.[95] Oswiu (r. 642-670) succeeded his brother after Penda killed the latter in 642. Oswiu made the monumental decision to orient his kingdom towards Latin Christianity at the Synod of Whitby in 664.[96] Oswiu called on the conference to settle, once and for all, the dispute between the Celtic and Latin Churches over the dating of Easter. The Northumbrian bishop Colman argued for the Insular side while Wilfrid, a Northumbrian priest educated in Rome, spoke for the Latin side. After hearing the arguments, Oswiu asked Colman whether it was true that God had given Peter the keys to heaven. Colman could not deny the verse in Matthew 16:18—the foundation of the Petrine doctrine which Pope Leo had forcefully posited some two centuries before. Oswiu ruled in favor of the Latin Church with the following reasoning,

> I also say unto you, that he is the door-keeper, and I will not gainsay him, but I desire, as far as I know and am able, in all things to obey his laws, lest haply when I come to the gates of the kingdom of Heaven, there should be none to open them, he being my adversary who is proved to have the keys.[97]

Oswiu's decision to favor Canterbury over Iona is interesting as most of the evidence suggests he favored Insular Christianity. Oswiu had deep ties with the Scots and was fluent in Gaelic. He was baptized by a Celtic churchman, and he was "instructed according to the doctrine of the Scots."[98] Evidence also suggests he spent some of his exile in Ireland as well.[99] A Scottish bishop sat at Lindisfarne at the time of the synod, and Northumbria was geographically closer to the Celtic regions of the north than to the Latin regions of the south. The Northumbrians enjoyed an above-average level of cultural, political, and social interaction with the Celtic populations on their western and northern borders.[100] Evidence demonstrates, for example, a diffusion of architectural forms between the Celts and the Northumbrians as well as similarities between the organization of Welsh and Northumbrian estates.[101] Oswiu's sister-in-law was a Pictish princess, and Oswiu himself took a British princess for one of his brides.[102] Moreover, ties between Northumbria and its Celtic neighbors ran deeper than the royal level. Native Britons integrated into Northumbrian society through their membership in several Northumbrian religious houses, and a large segment of the total Northumbrian population was of Celtic provenance.[103]

Political considerations may have affected Oswiu's decision more than any other factor. He was astute enough to see that the future rested with Latin Christianity and the pope in Rome, although the influence of his Latin Christian wife Eanflaed and the fresh memories of Cadwallon's atrocities could not have helped Bishop Colman's arguments at Whitby. The Synod marked the beginning of the end for Celtic Christianity in Britain. Thereafter, the Latin churchmen worked steadily to eradicate the unique practices of Insular Christianity from religious life.

Pope Gregory's mission to Kent turned out to be a resounding success. Latin Christianity was everywhere victorious less than a century and a half after Augustine and his fellow monks landed on the Isle of Thanet. The final bastion of paganism fell when the South Saxons converted in 681.[104] In 716, a Northumbrian priest named Egbert persuaded the monks of Iona to adopt the Roman date of Easter and the Roman style of tonsure.[105] The transition from paganism to Christianity was not an uninterrupted process. Most of the Anglo-Saxon kingdoms went through periods of apostasy depending on the current disposition of their rulers. However, Anglo-Saxon England, and indeed Britain as a whole, marched steadily towards the Roman Church after the conversion of Kent.

Notes

1. Leo the Great, "Sermon on His Birthday III: Delivered on the Anniversary of his Elevation to the Pontificate," in *A Select Library of Nicene and Post-Nicene Fathers of the Christian Church*, ed. Philip Schaff and Henry Wace, trans. Charles Lett Feltoe (New York, NY: The Christian Literature Company, 1895), 117.

2. Eusebius Pamphilus, "The Church History of Eusebius," in *A Select Library of the Nicene and Post-Nicene Fathers of the Christian Church*, ed. Philip Schaff and Henry Wace, trans. Arthur Cushman McGiffert, Church Fathers from the Fourth to the Eighth Century 2 (Grand Rapids, MI: W.M.B. Eerdmans Publishing Company, 1890), 1:1179-85.

3. Norman F. Cantor, *The Civilization of the Middle Ages* (New York, NY: Harper-Perennial, 1994), 58-62.

4. Gregory the Great, "Letter to John, Bishop of Constantinople," in *A Select Library of the Nicene and Post-Nicene Fathers of the Christian Church*, ed. Philip Schaff and Henry Wace, trans. James

Barmby, Church Fathers from the Fourth to the Eighth Century 2 (Grand Rapids, MI: W.M.B. Eerdmans Publishing Company, 1890), 12:730.

5. Justinian I, *Novella Constitutio* (n.p.: 536), 30.11, quoted in John Bagnell Bury, *History of the Later Roman Empire* (1923; repr., Mineola, NY: Dover, 1958), 2:26.

6. Gregory the Great, "Letter to Phocas, Emperor," in *A Select Library of the Nicene and Post-Nicene Fathers of the Christian Church*, ed. Philip Schaff and Henry Wace, trans. James Barmby, Church Fathers from the Fourth to the Eighth Century 2 (Grand Rapids, MI: W.M.B. Eerdmans Publishing Company, 1890), 13:239; Gregory the Great, "Letter to Constantina Augusta," in *A Select Library of the Nicene and Post-Nicene Fathers of the Christian Church*, ed. Philip Schaff and Henry Wace, trans. James Barmby, Church Fathers from the Fourth to the Eighth Century 2 (Grand Rapids, MI: W.M.B. Eerdmans Publishing Company, 1890), 12:967; Gregory the Great, "Letter to Eulogius, Bishop of Alexandria," in *A Select Library of the Nicene and Post-Nicene Fathers of the Christian Church*, ed. Philip Schaff and Henry Wace, trans. James Barmby, Church Fathers from the Fourth to the Eighth Century 2 (Grand Rapids, MI: W.M.B. Eerdmans Publishing Company, 1890), 12:1054.

7. Gregory the Great, "Letter to John, Bishop of Constantinople," in *A Select Library of the Nicene*, 12:730.

8. Gregory the Great, "Letter to Theodelinda, Queen of the Lombards," in *A Select Library of the Nicene and Post-Nicene Fathers of the Christian Church*, ed. Philip Schaff and Henry Wace, trans. James Barmby, Church Fathers from the Fourth to the Eighth Century 2 (Grand Rapids, MI: W.M.B. Eerdmans Publishing Company, 1890), 13:44.

9. Paul the Deacon, *Historia Langobardorum*, trans. William Dudley Foulke (Philadelphia, PA: University of Pennsylvania Press, 1907), 4.41.

10. Cantor, *The Civilization of the Middle Ages*, 58.

11. Gregory the Great, "Letter to Rechared, King of the Visigoths," in *A Select Library of the Nicene and Post-Nicene Fathers of the Christian Church*, ed. Philip Schaff and Henry Wace, trans. James Barmby, Church Fathers from the Fourth to the Eighth Century 2 (Grand Rapids, MI: W.M.B. Eerdmans Publishing Company, 1890), 13:93.

12. Ibid., 13:95-6.

13. Gregory the Great, "Letter to Claudius in Spain," in *A Select Library of the Nicene and Post-Nicene Fathers of the Christian Church*, ed. Philip Schaff and Henry Wace, trans. James Barmby, Church Fathers from the Fourth to the Eighth Century 2 (Grand Rapids, MI: W.M.B. Eerdmans Publishing Company, 1890), 13:90.

14. Gregory of Tours, *History of the Franks*, trans. Ernest Brehaut (New York, NY: Columbia University Press, 1916), 41.

15. Cantor, *The Civilization of the Middle Ages*, 94.

16. Ibid., 114-115.

17. Ibid., 116.

18. Gregory of Tours, *History of the Franks*, 105-6.

19. Gildas claimed that Christianity came in the first century during the reign of the Roman Emperor Tiberius, while Bede assigned the coming of Christianity to the second century. Bede claimed that the inhabitants of Britain preserved the Christian faith continuously until the persecutions of Diocletian. Dorothy Watts, whose *Religion in Late Roman Britain* was heavily informed by archaeological research, contends that Christianity was established in the second or early third century. The precise date of Christianity's arrival may be impossible to determine with absolute precision, but the presence of Christianity in Gaul by the second century meant that it was only a matter of time before

the underground religion was smuggled over to Britain. Gildas, "De Excidio Et Conquestu Britanniae," in *Six Old English Chronicles*, 8; Bede, *Historia Ecclesiastica Gentis Anglorum* [Ecclesiastical History of the English People], trans. John Allen Giles (London, GBR: Henry G. Bohn, 1859), 10; Dorothy Watts, *Religion in Late Roman Britain: Forces of Change* (London, GBR: Routledge, 2002), 2, 12-13.

20. Cantor, *The Civilization of the Middle Ages*, 93-4.

21. Tacitus, "Germania," in *Tacitus: The Agricola and Germania*, trans. R. B. Townshend (London, GBR: Methuen & Co., 1894), 65-68.

22. Jasper Ridley, *The History of England* (London, GBR: Routledge-Kegan Paul, 1981), 3.

23. Tacitus's account was probably colored by the traditional Roman contempt of the "wild other" across the frontiers, but it is the most contemporary one available. His insights into Germanic society are particularly valuable. The Germans, according to Tacitus, regarded it a "dull and stupid thing to painfully accumulate by sweat of the brow what might be won by a little blood." Given the emphasis which the Romans placed on the virtues of honest agriculture, it is easy to see why they detested the Germans as hopeless savages. Tacitus, "Germania," in *Tacitus: The Agricola and Germania*, 67-8.

24. Ridley, *The History of England*, 2.

25. Both Gildas and Bede levelled harsh criticisms against the Britons of the early-fifth century. Gildas scolded the Britons for being "neither brave in war nor in peace faithful," and Bede noted that the "cowardice of the Britons" only encouraged further Anglo-Saxon invasions. Gildas, "De Excidio Et Conquestu Britanniae," in *Six Old English Chronicles*, 6; Bede, *Historia Ecclesiastica Gentis Anglorum*, 1.15.

26. Barbara Yorke, *Kings and Kingdoms of Early Anglo-Saxon England* (London, GBR: Routledge-Taylor & Francis, 2003), 83.

27. This date is derived from Bede, *Historia Ecclesiastica Gentis Anglorum*, 1.25.

28. An overall trend of political consolidation prevailed throughout the Anglo-Saxon period as smaller states were accreted into the orbit of larger ones, and by the early ninth century there stood only four large kingdoms: Wessex, Mercia, Northumbria, and East Anglia. The decentralized political structure of Anglo-Saxon Britain was finally destroyed by the Danish invasion of the mid-ninth century. For a chronology of the Danish invasion, see J. A. Giles, trans., *The Anglo-Saxon Chronicle* (London, GBR: Henry G. Bohn, 1859), 341-52.

29. More moderate interpretations of the Anglo-Saxon invasion have been floated in recent years. Barbara Yorke downplays the impact of the Anglo-Saxon invasions on the economy and society of Roman Britain, contending that the physical, social, and religious deterioration of the island was already well underway before the Anglo-Saxons arrived. She blames the simplification of Romano-British society in the years leading up to the Roman collapse on the complex problems of the declining Roman Empire. Yorke, *Kings and Kingdoms*, 1-9. Similarly, Dorothy Watts claimed that Christianity failed to become fully established in Britain owing to a resurgence of Celtic paganism, the pre-Roman religion of the island, after the apostasy of the Emperor Julian. She contends that British resistance to Romanization throughout the centuries of occupation reinforced this development. If this is true, the impact of the Anglo-Saxon invasion on Christianity may not have been as dramatic as it is often portrayed to be. Watts, *Religion in Late Roman Britain*, 24-95.

30. Thomas Cahill said it best when he wrote, "While Rome and its ancient empire faded from memory and a new, illiterate Europe rose on its ruins, a vibrant, literary culture was blooming in secret along its Celtic fringe." Thomas Cahill, *How the Irish Saved Civilization* (New York, NY: Anchor Books, 1995), 183.

31. Patrick called the place "the end of the earth, where now my littleness is seen." Saint Patrick, "Confessio," in *The Writings of St. Patrick, the Apostle of Ireland*, 3rd ed., trans. Charles H. H.

Wright (London, GBR: Religious Tract Society, 1894), 47, 53; J. B. Bury, *The Life of Saint Patrick and His Place in History* (London, GBR: Macmillan, 1905), 26-28.

32. On this Patrick wrote, "I prayed frequently during the day; love of God and the fear of Him increased more and more, and faith became stronger. . . . In one day I said about a hundred prayers, and in the night nearly the same." Saint Patrick, "Confessio," in *The Writings of St. Patrick*, 53.

33. J. B. Bury places the date of his death at 461. Bury, *The Life of Saint Patrick*, 206; Ridley, *The History of England*, 6.

34. Patrick himself admits his lack of education. Saint Patrick, "Confessio," in *The Writings of St. Patrick*, 49, 67.

35. Charles H. H. Wright, *The Writings of St. Patrick, the Apostle of Ireland*, 3rd ed. (London, GBR: Religious Tract Society, 1894), 23-25.

36. The Scots themselves were Irish immigrants who had come to south-west Pictland in Patrick's time. Bede, *Historia Ecclesiastica Gentis Anglorum*, 3.4.

37. The Ionan monks had established no less than sixty monastic communities in Columba's name by the time of his death in the late-sixth century. Bede, *Historia Ecclesiastica Gentis Anglorum*, 3.4; Cahill, *How the Irish Saved Civilization*, 184-5.

38. Bede, *Historia Ecclesiastica Gentis Anglorum*, 3.3.

39. Ibid., 3.3, 3.5.

40. Ibid.

41. It is telling that Bede, a fierce partisan of Latin Christianity, lavished praise on the Irish churchmen for their "continence, love of God, and observance of monastic rules" and their "piety and chastity" in spite of the fact that they "employed doubtful cycles in fixing the time of the great festival [of Easter]." He excuses their unorthodoxy, asserting that their remoteness prevented anyone from bringing them the "synodal decrees for the observance of Easter." Bede, *Historia Ecclesiastica Gentis Anglorum*, 3.4.

42. Ibid., 3.4.

43. Cantor, *The Civilization of the Middle Ages*, 163. The conspicuous absence of dioceses reflects the isolated development of Irish Christianity. Dioceses initially followed the provincial outlines of the Roman Empire, but Rome had never exercised control in Ireland. Therefore, the Irish Church had no territorial framework to use as a model. William E. Dunstan, *Ancient Rome* (Lanham, MD: Rowman & Littlefield Publishers, Inc., 2010), 483.

44. Ignatius, bishop of Antioch in the second century, claimed that "he that honoureth the bishop is honoured of God; he that doeth aught without the knowledge of the bishop rendereth service to the devil." Ignatius, "Epistle to the Smyrneans," in *The Apostolic Fathers*, 2nd ed., trans. J. B. Lightfoot (New York, NY: Macmillan, 1889), 2:569-70.

45. The Eastern Greek elements within Irish Christianity came from the throngs of Christian immigrants who escaped to Ireland in the wake of the Germanic invasions. Ireland experienced an influx of fleeing ascetics, monks, and other holy men after Patrick's time, and many of these came from the Roman provinces in the Near East. Cahill, *How the Irish Saved Civilization*, 180; Cantor, *The Civilization of the Middle Ages*, 145-9, 162.

46. The precise appearance of Insular tonsure can only be guessed at, but Daniel McCarthy offers some suggestions. See Daniel McCarthy, "On the Shape of the Insular Tonsure," *Celtica* 24 (2003): 140-67; Bede, *Historia Ecclesiastica Gentis Anglorum*, 5.21-22.

47. Ibid., 3.4, 3.3, 2.4, 2.19, 3.25, 5.21-22.

48. For an example of such an appeal, see Bede, *Historia Ecclesiastica Gentis Anglorum*, 2.19.

49. Cahill, *How the Irish Saved Civilization*, 188-9.

50. Columbanus, "Letter to Pope Gregory," in *A Select Library of the Nicene and Post-Nicene Fathers of the Christian Church*, ed. Philip Schaff and Henry Wace, trans. James Barmby, Church Fathers from the Fourth to the Eighth Century 2 (Grand Rapids, MI: W. M. B. Eerdmans Publishing Company, 1890), 13:101-8.

51. Cahill, *How the Irish Saved Civilization*, 191.

52. Bede, *Historia Ecclesiastica Gentis Anglorum*, 2.1.

53. Gregory the Great, "Letter to Candidus, Presbyter," in *A Select Library of the Nicene and Post-Nicene Fathers of the Christian Church*, ed. Philip Schaff and Henry Wace, trans. James Barmby, Church Fathers from the Fourth to the Eighth Century 2 (Grand Rapids, MI: W.M.B. Eerdmans Publishing Company, 1890), 12:1010.

54. Bede, *Historia Ecclesiastica Gentis Anglorum*, 1.23.

55. Gregory the Great, "Selected Epistles of the Fourteenth Indiction," in *A Select Library of the Nicene and Post-Nicene Fathers of the Christian Church*, ed. Philip Schaff and Henry Wace, trans. James Barmby, Church Fathers from the Fourth to the Eighth Century 2 (Grand Rapids, MI: W.M.B. Eerdmans Publishing Company, 1890), 12:1046-55; Bede, *Historia Ecclesiastica Gentis Anglorum*, 1.24.

56. Gregory the Great, "Letter to Clotaire, King of the Franks," in *A Select Library of the Nicene and Post-Nicene Fathers of the Christian Church*, ed. Philip Schaff and Henry Wace, trans. James Barmby Church Fathers from the Fourth to the Eighth Century 2 (Grand Rapids, MI: W.M.B. Eerdmans Publishing Company, 1890), 13:179; Gregory the Great, "Letter to Brunichild, Queen of the Franks," in *A Select Library of the Nicene and Post-Nicene Fathers of the Christian Church*, ed. Philip Schaff and Henry Wace, trans. James Barmby, Church Fathers from the Fourth to the Eighth Century 2 (Grand Rapids, MI: W.M.B. Eerdmans Publishing Company, 1890), 13:180; Gregory the Great, "Letter to Syagrius, Bishop of Augustodunum," in *A Select Library of the Nicene and Post-Nicene Fathers of the Christian Church*, ed. Philip Schaff and Henry Wace, trans. James Barmby, Church Fathers from the Fourth to the Eighth Century 2 (Grand Rapids, MI: W.M.B. Eerdmans Publishing Company, 1890), 13:77.

57. Bede, *Historia Ecclesiastica Gentis Anglorum*, 1.25.

58. Ibid.

59. Ibid.

60. Ibid., 1.26.

61. Ibid.

62. Ibid.

63. Gregory the Great, "Letter to Eulogius, Bishop of Alexandria," in *A Select Library of the Nicene and Post-Nicene Fathers of the Christian Church*, ed. Philip Schaff and Henry Wace, trans. James Barmby, Church Fathers from the Fourth to the Eighth Century 2 (Grand Rapids, MI: W.M.B. Eerdmans Publishing Company, 1890), 12:1132.

64. Bede, *Historia Ecclesiastica Gentis Anglorum*, 1.27.

65. Ibid., 2.2.

66. Ibid.

67. Ibid.

68. Ibid.

69. Yorke, *Kings and Kingdoms*, 83.

70. Cantor, *The Civilization of the Middle Ages*, 162.

71. Bede, *Historia Ecclesiastica Gentis Anglorum*, 2.14.

72. Ibid., 3.1.

73. Ibid., 2.20.

74. Ibid., 3.1.

75. Ibid., 2.2.

76. Ibid., 2.20.

77. Ibid., 1.29.

78. Bede, *Historia Ecclesiastica Gentis Anglorum*, 1.27; Gregory the Great, "Letter to Augustine, Bishop of the Angli," in *A Select Library of the Nicene and Post-Nicene Fathers of the Christian Church*, ed. Philip Schaff and Henry Wace, trans. James Barmby, Church Fathers from the Fourth to the Eighth Century 2 (Grand Rapids, MI: W.M.B. Eerdmans Publishing Company, 1890), 13:184.

79. Gregory the Great, "Letter to Edilbert, King of the Angli," in *A Select Library of the Nicene and Post-Nicene Fathers of the Christian Church*, ed. Philip Schaff and Henry Wace, trans. James Barmby, Church Fathers from the Fourth to the Eighth Century 2 (Grand Rapids, MI: W.M.B. Eerdmans Publishing Company, 1890), 13:196; Bede, *Historia Ecclesiastica Gentis Anglorum*, 1.32.

80. Yorke, *Kings and Kingdoms*, 47-8; Bede, *Historia Ecclesiastica Gentis Anglorum*, 1.33.

81. Bede, *Historia Ecclesiastica Gentis Anglorum*, 2.15.

82. Ibid., 3.24.

83. Ibid., 3.7.

84. Ibid.

85. Ibid., 2.9.

86. Ibid.

87. Ibid., 2.10-11.

88. Ibid., 2.14.

89. Ibid., 2.11.

90. Gregory the Great, "Letter to Bertha, Queen of the Angli," in *A Select Library of the Nicene and Post-Nicene Fathers of the Christian Church*, ed. Philip Schaff and Henry Wace, trans.

James Barmby, Church Fathers from the Fourth to the Eighth Century 2 (Grand Rapids, MI: W.M.B. Eerdmans Publishing Company, 1890), 13:141.

91. Gregory the Great, "Letter to Theodelinda, Queen of the Lombards," in *A Select Library*, 13:44; Gregory the Great, "Letter to Theodelinda, Queen of the Lombards," in *A Select Library of the Nicene and Post-Nicene Fathers of the Christian Church*, ed. Philip Schaff and Henry Wace, trans. James Barmby, Church Fathers from the Fourth to the Eighth Century 2 (Grand Rapids, MI: W.M.B. Eerdmans Publishing Company, 1890), 13:253.

92. Paul the Deacon, *Historia Langobardorum*, 4.6.

93. Gregory of Tours, *History of the Franks*, 39-41.

94. Bede, *Historia Ecclesiastica Gentis Anglorum*, 3.1, 3.3.

95. Ibid., 3.1.

96. Ibid., 3.25.

97. Ibid.

98. Ibid., 3.25, 3.1.

99. Yorke, *Kings and Kingdoms*, 85.

100. Ibid., 83-6.

101. Ibid.

102. Ibid., 85.

103. Ibid., 86.

104. Bede, *Historia Ecclesiastica Gentis Anglorum*, 4.13.

105. Bede, *Historia Ecclesiastica Gentis Anglorum*, 5.22, 3.4. The Scots and the Picts were persuaded to adopt the Roman custom of tonsure and Easter earlier in the eighth century. See Bede, *Historia Ecclesiastica Gentis Anglorum*, 5.15, 5.21. The British Christians of Wales and Cornwall still refused to abandon their Celtic practices as of Bede's final entry in 731, but Bede dismissed these nations as politically weak and rapidly losing their independence to their English neighbors to the east. Bede, *Historia Ecclesiastica Gentis Anglorum*, 5.23.

Bibliography

The Anglo-Saxon Chronicle. Translated by J. A. Giles. London, GBR: Henry G. Bohn, 1859.

Bede. *Historia Ecclesiastica Gentis Anglorum* [Ecclesiastical History of the English People]. Translated by John Allen Giles. London, GBR: Henry G. Bohn, 1859.

Bury, J. B. *The Life of Saint Patrick and His Place in History*. London, GBR: Macmillan, 1905.

Cahill, Thomas. *How the Irish Saved Civilization*. New York, NY: Anchor Books, 1995.

Cantor, Norman F. *The Civilization of the Middle Ages*. New York, NY: Harper-Perennial, 1994.

Columbanus. "Letter to Pope Gregory." In *A Select Library of the Nicene and Post-Nicene Fathers of the Christian Church*, edited by Philip Schaff and Henry Wace. Translated by James Barmby. Vol. 13. Church Fathers from the Fourth to the Eighth Century 2, 101-8. Grand Rapids, MI: W. M. B. Eerdmans Publishing Company, 1890.

Dunstan, William E. *Ancient Rome*. Lanham, MD: Rowman & Littlefield Publishers, Inc., 2010.

Gelasius I. "Letter of Pope Gelasius I to Emperor Anastasius on the Superiority of the Spiritual over the Temporal Power." In *Readings in European History*, edited by James Harvey Robinson. Vol. 1, 72-73. New York, NY: Ginn & Company, 1904.

Gildas. "De Excidio Et Conquestu Britanniae." In *Six Old English Chronicles*. Translated by John Allen Giles, 8. London, GBR: G. Bell & Sons, 1891.

Giles, J. A., trans. *The Anglo-Saxon Chronicle*. London, GBR: Henry G. Bohn, 1859.

Gregory of Tours. *History of the Franks*. Translated by Ernest Brehaut. New York, NY: Columbia University Press, 1916.

Gregory the Great. "Letter to Augustine, Bishop of the Angli." In *A Select Library of the Nicene and Post-Nicene Fathers of the Christian Church*, edited by Philip Schaff and Henry Wace. Translated by James Barmby. Vol. 13. Church Fathers from the Fourth to the Eighth Century 2, 184. Grand Rapids, MI: W.M.B. Eerdmans Publishing Company, 1890.

———. "Letter to Bertha, Queen of the Angli." In *A Select Library of the Nicene and Post-Nicene Fathers of the Christian Church*, edited by Philip Schaff and Henry Wace. Translated by James Barmby. Vol. 13. Church Fathers from the Fourth to the Eighth Century 2, 141. Grand Rapids, MI: W.M.B. Eerdmans Publishing Company, 1890.

———. "Letter to Brunichild, Queen of the Franks." In *A Select Library of the Nicene and Post-Nicene Fathers of the Christian Church*, edited by Philip Schaff and Henry Wace. Translated by James Barmby. Vol. 13. Church Fathers from the Fourth to the Eighth Century 2, 180. Grand Rapids, MI: W.M.B. Eerdmans Publishing Company, 1890.

———. "Letter to Candidus, Presbyter." In *A Select Library of the Nicene and Post-Nicene Fathers of the Christian Church*, edited by Philip Schaff and Henry Wace. Translated by James Barmby. Vol. 12. Church Fathers from the Fourth to the Eighth Century 2, 1010. Grand Rapids, MI: W.M.B. Eerdmans Publishing Company, 1890.

———. "Letter to Claudius in Spain." In *A Select Library of the Nicene and Post-Nicene Fathers of the Christian Church*, edited by Philip Schaff and Henry Wace. Translated by James Barmby. Vol. 13. Church Fathers from the Fourth to the Eighth Century 2, 90. Grand Rapids, MI: W.M.B. Eerdmans Publishing Company, 1890.

———. "Letter to Clotaire, King of the Franks." In *A Select Library of the Nicene and Post-Nicene Fathers of the Christian Church*, edited by Philip Schaff and Henry Wace. Translated by James Barmby. Vol. 13. Church Fathers from the Fourth to the Eighth Century 2, 179. Grand Rapids, MI: W.M.B. Eerdmans Publishing Company, 1890.

———. "Letter to Constantina Augusta." In *A Select Library of the Nicene and Post-Nicene Fathers of the Christian Church*, edited by Philip Schaff and Henry Wace. Translated by James Barmby. Vol. 12. Church Fathers from the Fourth to the Eighth Century 2, 967. Grand Rapids, MI: W.M.B. Eerdmans Publishing Company, 1890.

———. "Letter to Edilbert, King of the Angli." In *A Select Library of the Nicene and Post-Nicene Fathers of the Christian Church*, edited by Philip Schaff and Henry Wace. Translated by James Barmby. Vol. 13. Church Fathers from the Fourth to the Eighth Century 2, 196. Grand Rapids, MI: W.M.B. Eerdmans Publishing Company, 1890.

———. "Letter to Eulogius, Bishop of Alexandria." In *A Select Library of the Nicene and Post-Nicene Fathers of the Christian Church*, edited by Philip Schaff and Henry Wace. Translated by James Barmby. Vol. 12. Church Fathers from the Fourth to the Eighth Century 2, 1054. Grand Rapids, MI: W.M.B. Eerdmans Publishing Company, 1890.

———. "Letter to Eulogius, Bishop of Alexandria." In *A Select Library of the*

Nicene and Post-Nicene Fathers of the Christian Church, edited by Philip Schaff and Henry Wace. Translated by James Barmby. Vol. 12. Church Fathers from the Fourth to the Eighth Century 2, 1132. Grand Rapids, MI: W.M.B. Eerdmans Publishing Company, 1890.

_____. "Letter to John, Bishop of Constantinople." In *A Select Library of the Nicene and Post-Nicene Fathers of the Christian Church*, edited by Philip Schaff and Henry Wace. Translated by James Barmby. Vol. 12. Church Fathers from the Fourth to the Eighth Century 2, 730. Grand Rapids, MI: W.M.B. Eerdmans Publishing Company, 1890.

_____. "Letter to Phocas, Emperor." In *A Select Library of the Nicene and Post-Nicene Fathers of the Christian Church*, edited by Philip Schaff and Henry Wace. Translated by James Barmby. Vol. 13. Church Fathers from the Fourth to the Eighth Century 2, 239. Grand Rapids, MI: W.M.B. Eerdmans Publishing Company, 1890.

_____. "Letter to Rechared, King of the Visigoths." In *A Select Library of the Nicene and Post-Nicene Fathers of the Christian Church*, edited by Philip Schaff and Henry Wace. Translated by James Barmby. Vol. 13. Church Fathers from the Fourth to the Eighth Century 2, 93. Grand Rapids, MI: W.M.B. Eerdmans Publishing Company, 1890.

_____. "Letter to Syagrius, Bishop of Augustodunum." In *A Select Library of the Nicene and Post-Nicene Fathers of the Christian Church*, edited by Philip Schaff and Henry Wace. Translated by James Barmby. Vol. 13. Church Fathers from the Fourth to the Eighth Century 2, 77. Grand Rapids, MI: W.M.B. Eerdmans Publishing Company, 1890.

_____. "Letter to Theodelinda, Queen of the Lombards." In *A Select Library of the Nicene and Post-Nicene Fathers of the Christian Church*, edited by Philip Schaff and Henry Wace. Translated by James Barmby. Vol. 13. Church Fathers from the Fourth to the Eighth Century 2, 44. Grand Rapids, MI: W.M.B. Eerdmans Publishing Company, 1890.

_____. "Letter to Theodelinda, Queen of the Lombards." In *A Select Library of the Nicene and Post-Nicene Fathers of the Christian Church*, edited by Philip Schaff and Henry Wace. Translated by James Barmby. Vol. 13. Church Fathers from the Fourth to the Eighth Century 2, 253. Grand Rapids, MI: W.M.B. Eerdmans Publishing Company, 1890.

_____. "Selected Epistles of the Fourteenth Indiction." In *A Select Library of the Nicene and Post-Nicene Fathers of the Christian Church*, edited by Philip Schaff and Henry Wace. Translated by James Barmby. Vol. 12. Church Fathers from the Fourth to the Eighth Century 2, 1046-55. Grand Rapids, MI: W.M.B. Eerdmans Publishing Company, 1890.

Ignatius. "Epistle to the Smyrneans." In *The Apostolic Fathers*. 2nd ed. Translated by

J. B. Lightfoot. Vol. 2, 569-70. New York, NY: Macmillan, 1889.

Justinian I. *Novella Constitutio*. N.p.: 536. Quoted in Bury, John Bagnell. *History of the Later Roman Empire*. 1923. Vol. 2. Reprint, Mineola, NY: Dover, 1958.

Leo the Great. "Sermon on His Birthday III: Delivered on the Anniversary of his Elevation to the Pontificate." In *A Select Library of Nicene and Post-Nicene Fathers of the Christian Church*, edited by Philip Schaff and Henry Wace. Translated by Charles Lett Feltoe, 117. New York, NY: The Christian Literature Company, 1895.

McCarthy, Daniel. "On the Shape of the Insular Tonsure." *Celtica* 24 (2003): 140 -67.

Pamphilus, Eusebius. "The Church History of Eusebius." In *A Select Library of the Nicene and Post-Nicene Fathers of the Christian Church*, edited by Philip Schaff and Henry Wace. Translated by Arthur Cushman McGiffert. Vol. 1. Church Fathers from the Fourth to the Eighth Century 2, 1179-85. Grand Rapids, MI: W.M.B. Eerdmans Publishing Company, 1890.

Paul the Deacon. *Historia Langobardorum*. Translated by William Dudley Foulke. Philadelphia, PA: University of Pennsylvania Press, 1907.

Ridley, Jasper. *The History of England*. London, GBR: Routledge-Kegan Paul, 1981.

Saint Patrick. "Confessio." In *The Writings of St. Patrick, the Apostle of Ireland*. 3rd ed. Translated by Charles H. H. Wright, 47. London, GBR: Religious Tract Society, 1894.

Tacitus. "Germania." In *Tacitus: The Agricola and Germania*. Translated by R. B. Townshend, 65-68. London, GBR: Methuen & Co., 1894.

Thompson, E. A. *Saint Germanus of Auxerre and the End of Roman Britain*. Suffolk, GBR: Boydell Press, 1984.

Watts, Dorothy. *Religion in Late Roman Britain: Forces of Change*. London, GBR: Routledge, 2002.

Wright, Charles H. H. *The Writings of St. Patrick, the Apostle of Ireland*. 3rd ed. London, GBR: Religious Tract Society, 1894.

Yorke, Barbara. *Kings and Kingdoms of Early Anglo-Saxon England*. London, GBR: Routledge-Taylor & Francis, 2003.

Charles Martel Turns South:
The Hammer's Campaigns in Southern France 733-737

Patrick S. Baker

Introduction

In 732, Charles Martel defeated the Muslim Moors at the Battle of Tours and stopped the Islamic advance into Western Europe. The victory won him the cognomen Martel or "hammer" for the way he pounded his enemies. In addition to this title, his peers recognized him as the Mayor of the Palace and Prince of the Franks. With the Islamic advance halted, Charles Martel turned his strategic efforts to securing the city of Narbonne and the rest of modern-day southern France. From 720 to 732, he had campaigned extensively throughout what is today northern France, Germany, and the Benelux countries. After 732 until his death in 741, Charles Martel campaigned, almost exclusively, in Aquitaine, southern Burgundy around Lyon, the Rhone Valley to the Mediterranean Sea, and in Septimania, modern-day Languedoc.[1]

Before 732, Charles Martel's primary interest was in establishing himself as the principal leader of the three Frankish kingdoms of Austrasia, Neustria, and Burgundy. After 732, he shifted his strategic focus southward. Charles Martel's southern strategy was the result of a Moorish-controlled Narbonne. From there they threatened Frankish interests in the Rhone Valley, southern Burgundy, and Aquitaine. To secure his realm, Charles Martel had to eliminate the Moors from what is today southern France.[2]

Historiography

The primary sources regarding Martel's move south are a collection of medieval chronicles, histories, and annals primarily written in Latin. For the most part, these works are anonymous. The most important are *The Fourth Book of the Chronicle of Fredegar with its Continuations*, likely completed in 768, the *Annales Mettenses Priores* (The Earlier Annals of Metz) compiled about 805, Paul the Deacon's *History of the Lombards* completed in the late Eighth Century, the *Liber Historiae Francorum* (The Book of the History of the Franks) completed in 727, the *Chronicon Moissiacense* (The Chronicle of Moissac) composed sometime in the ninth century, and *The Royal Frankish Annals*, likely edited into a final form in the mid-800s. All these works, written some years after the events, used earlier written sources and oral traditions. The *Monumenta Germaniae Historica* (Monument to German History) is a collection of early medieval texts edited and published in a massive set of over ninety volumes.[3]

For information regarding the Moors, *The Chronicle of 754*, sometimes referred to as the *Mozarabic Chronicle of 754,* is a singularly important source. A Christian, possibly a churchman, composed the Latin *Chronicle of 754* in Moslem Spain. This chronicle, translated and edited by Kenneth Baxter Wolf in 1990, gives a great deal of information about Spain under the Moors and their conflict with the Franks. Other valuable information is contained in Arab sources that are available in either French or English translations. Muhammad Al-Makkari's *The History of the Mohammedan Dynasties in Spain in 2 Volumes,* completed sometime before the author's death in 1632, is a compilation of earlier written material, much of which is now lost. This work was translated into English by Pascual de Gayangos in 1840 (Volume 1) and 1843 (Volume 2). Making use of now lost sources, 'Izz al-Dīn Ibn Al-Athir completed The *Prefect History* in the 1220s. E. Fagnan extracted, edited, and translated into French the sections regarding North Africa and Spain as *Annales du Maghreb et de l'Espagne,* published in 1901. Ibn Al-Qutiya's *Early Islamic Spain: the History of Ibn al-Qutiya* completed between 961 and 977 records much of the oral tradition about the Moors' early years in Spain. David James translated the work into English in 2009.[4]

Their brevity often mars the value of the above sources. Oftentimes, a few short lines cover the events of entire years. Furthermore, the "facts" presented in the chronicles cannot always be taken at face value. For example, in his *History of the Lombards*, Paul the Deacon reports that Charles Martel and Eudo, Duke of Aquitaine, fought together at the Battle of Toulouse and killed over 300,000 Moors. Paul confuses the 721 Battle of Toulouse with the 732 Battle of Tours. In addition, the number of Moors reported killed is at least an order of magnitude larger than the greatest possible number of the entire Moorish army involved in the battle.[5]

Many of the Latin primary sources, specifically the *Fourth Book of the Chronicle of Fredegar with its Continuations*, the *Annales Mettenses Priores,* the *Liber Historiae Francorum* and *The Royal Frankish Annals* are unabashedly pro-Frank and pro-Carolingian and are nearly hagiographic in their praise of Charles Martel and his descendants. Christian and Muslim sources are also biased. Ibn Al-Athir's, Al-Qutiya's and Al-Makkari's works are all pro-Muslim. Clearly, none of these sources contains objective writing. Therefore, critical reading is necessary.[6]

Many secondary works explore the military organization, strategy, tactics, weapons, and motivations of the two sides as they battled for control of what is now southeastern France. For discussions of the Frankish military and political organization Bernard S. Bachrach's *Merovingian Military Organization, 481-751* (1972) and *Early Carolingian Warfare: Prelude to Empire* (2001) are invaluable. Also, Paul Fouracre's *The Age of Charles Martel* (2000) is extremely useful for information on the Frankish realm and Charles Martel. Important secondary sources about Muslims such as *The Arab Conquest of Spain, 710-797* (1989) by Roger Collins and Hugh Kennedy's *The Armies of the Caliphs: Military and Society in the Early Islamic State* (2001) are equally valuable for information on the caliphates' military organization and the internal politics of *al -Andalus*.

The Theater of War

Franks in Francia

The year 732 marked three hundred years of established Frankish kingdoms in Gaul. The Franks first entered Gaul as Roman auxiliaries and fought the Huns at Chalon in 451. Since then, under the Merovingian kings, the Franks had, at one time or the other, either directly ruled or had formed allied or client relationships with regions from Bavaria to Gascony. However, outside the central kingdoms of Austrasia, Neustria, and Burgundy this control oscillated between direct rule and no control at all. [7]

This period was known as the time of the *rois faineants* or "Do Nothing" kings. Power centered on the *Maior Domaus*, or Mayor of the Palace. The kings remained in their position as figureheads. Though a selection process existed amongst the nobles, the death of the Mayor of the Palace often produced power struggles. Bloodlines did not guarantee the office. As a result, assassinations, a coup, or outright war decided the matter.[8]

Charles Martel was the third son of Pippin the Middle, the Austrasian Mayor of the Palace. In 715, Charles's stepmother imprisoned him to prevent him from inheriting his father's position and passed favor onto his infant nephews. However, Charles Martel managed to escape. With the Austrasian Carolingian clan defeated and the family treasure handed over the rival Neustrians, Charles Martel organized a counterstroke against the Neustrians at Ambl.eve near Malmedy. He ambushed and inflicted a serious defeat on them just one year after escaping his confinement.[9]

Charles Martel went on to defeat his Neustrian rival, Ragamfred, again in 717 at Vichy. In 718, Charles Martel chased an army of Aquitainians, allied to Ragamfred, back over the River Loire. Later that same year he marched east of the River Rhine and defeated the rebellious Saxons. By 724, Charles Martel was the master of *Francia*. He began to reassert control over regions that had slipped loose from the *regnum Francorum* (Kingdom of the Franks) during the preceding years.[10]

Despite the chaotic conditions, the Frankish homeland was surprisingly secure, stable, and expansive when compared to other successor states of the old Western Roman Empire. The reason for this is rooted in "the Frankish System" of rule. Even on the periphery of the realm, Frankish rulers operated through local power structures when they could, and sought consensus among the powerful magnates for important decisions. The rulers called meetings of these powerful men, sometimes at the start of the campaign season as a military muster, but also at other times to discuss issues important to the realm. Consensus was an important aspect of the Frankish political system. Failure to engage in dialogue often disrupted the system.[11]

Moors in al-Andalus

The Muslims, or Moors, as they were known to the Franks, were newcomers to the continent. In fact they were a new force in the world. Motivated by a new religion, Islam, the small, fierce Arab tribes had emerged from the desert and through conversion and conquest had, by 711, ruled half the known world. In the west, the Muslims stood on the south shore of the Straits of Gibraltar and looked north at the Visigoth kingdom of Hispania, modern day Spain and Portugal. Meanwhile, in the east they were fast approaching the gates of Constantinople.[12]

The Umayyad Caliphate was under a political and religious mandate to take new lands and *Hispania* was the next logical step of expansion after the conquest of the Berbers of North Africa. However, there is a myth about the Muslim invasion of *Hispania*. The tale involves the daughter of a powerful Visigoth noble raped by Roderic, the last Visigoth King of *Hispania*, and in revenge for the crime, the girl's father invited the Muslims into Spain.[13]

Either way, the conquest of *Hispania* was swift. Before the main invasion, the Muslims in North Africa scouted, raided, and pillaged the southern coast of Spain. In 711, Tariq ibn Ziyad arrived in *Hispania* with a force of about seven thousand men for the Battle of Guadalete, the only large battle fought between the Muslim invaders and the Visigoth army. The Moors almost completely annihilated the Visigoths. A few Visigoth survivors fled. A civil war and a conspiracy within Roderick's government weakened the Visigoths' resistance to the Moors. Rivals for the Visigoth throne ultimately betrayed the king.[14]

An additional force of twelve thousand men led by Musa ibn Nusayr joined Tariq for clean-up operations. Thereafter, large-scale resistance ended. However, some cities continued to resist. Musa besieged, looted, and burned those cities. Musa and Tariq advanced as far east as Zaragoza. Musa, recalled to Damascus, took Tariq with him, but left his son, Abd al-Aziz ibn Musa, in charge of the newly conquered territory.[15]

Abd al-Aziz continued the pacification of the peninsula "by subduing several important fortresses and cities."[16] However, he was just as happy to sign treaties with local Visigoth nobles; which followed the tradition of similar pacts signed by the Muslims in their earlier conquests. In 713, Abd al-Aziz signed a treaty with the Visigoth nobleman, Theodemir, called Tudmir by the Moors, in which the Muslim leader promised to respect Christian property and religion and vowed to recognize Theodemir's sovereignty. In return, the Visigoth noble would not hide deserters, would pay an annual per capita tax of hard money, and would provide certain agricultural goods. Arrangements like this treaty allowed the small Muslim armies to deal with armed rebellions and at the same time expand their sphere of influence. These treaty arrangements were so beneficial to both sides that they maintained them for years. [17]

The Theater of the Conflict

Septimania

Septimania was the part of the Visigoth kingdom of Hispania that extended east of the Pyrenees along the Mediterranean coast, nearly to the Rhone River, and on the north along a line between the cities of Carcassonne and Toulouse. Septimania's capital was Narbonne. Other important cities were Nimes, Maguelone, Agde, and Beziers. By 507, the Franks destroyed the Visigoth kingdom of Toulouse and occupied all of its territory, except Septimania. A series of back and forth wars in the early 500s saw the Franks take all of the Visigoth territory only to be dislodged again before 548. After the last campaign, the territory remained part of the Visigoth kingdom. [18]

Following the Muslim invasion of Spain in 711, Septimania, under a Visigoth king named Ardo, maintained some autonomy. However, independence did not last long. In 717, the Moors crossed the Pyrenees Mountains and engaged the Visigoths in frequent skirmishes. By 720, the Muslims occupied Narbonne, and were soon using it as a raiding base. [19]

From 720 to 759, the Moors saw Septimania as an integrated part of the Caliphate, just like the rest of al-Andalus (Muslim Spain). Furthermore, for two generations, the city of Narbonne was a valuable strategic asset of the Moors. From this stronghold, the Moors launched raids up the Rhone Valley, into Aquitaine, and along the Mediterranean coast, without having to navigate the difficult mountain passes. As such, Narbonne was a primary strategic target for the Franks.[20]

Aquitaine

Aquitaine, in the eighth century, was a rough pentagon, bound on the southwest by the Pyrenees, by Biscayne Bay to the west, the Loire River on the north and northeast, and an ill-defined line about halfway between Toulouse and Carcassonne on the south. The Frankish king Clovis, in an alliance with the Byzantine Empire, shattered the Visigoth kingdom of Toulouse in 507 at the Battle of Vouille. After Clovis's victory, Aquitaine became a somewhat troublesome part of the Frankish realms. Sometimes Aquitaine appeared to be an integrated part of the Frankish realms and other times nearly completely independent. Only a long series of campaigns by Charles Martel, his son, King Pippin I, and his grandson, Charlemagne, brought Aquitaine under complete control. Until then, the region enjoyed a singularly ambiguous political situation.[21]

A number of Frankish kings and queens controlled parts of the region through most of the sixth century. However, after 567, the cities of Aquitaine passed on as an inheritance in a rapid and apparently random fashion to a number of rulers. For example, in a span of just twenty years, five kings and two queens held the city of Cahors. Because of unstable leadership, Aquitaine remained politically disjointed in the late sixth and early seventh centuries.[22]

When Dagobert I inherited the entire kingdom from his father in 628, Dagobert's half-brother, Charibert, tried to seize the throne. However, "Charibert … made little headway since he was simple-minded." Rather than kill his half-brother, Dagobert gave him Aquitaine from the Loire River to the Pyrenees Mountains. This included the cities of Toulouse, Cahors, Agen, Perigueux, and Saintes. In exchange for this generous land grant, Charibert would make no further claims to any other part of his father's kingdom. During his reign, Charibert extended his rule by conquering Gascony, roughly the area between the River Garonne and the Pyrenees along the Atlantic coast. Charibert died in the ninth year of Dagobert's reign, and his infant son, Chilperic, died shortly after his father. These deaths drew some suspicion that Dagobert had arranged the assassination of both. The death of Chilperic returned the Kingdom of the Frank to single rule.[23]

In the confusion that beset Francia in the late 600s, civil war raged in Neustria, open war broke out between Neustria and Austrasia, and at least two kings died a violent death. Aquitaine reclaimed a measure of political, military, and cultural independence from the Kingdom of the Franks. In 691, Pippin the Middle took sole leadership of the Franks. The Aquitainians along with the Saxons, Bavarians, Bretons and other peoples had managed to break away from Frankish rule. During this time, the Aquitainians also reasserted a certain cultural distinctiveness from the Franks. For example, the Franks referred to the peoples that lived south of the Loire as "Romans." In contrast, the Aquitainians called the Franks that resided north of the Loire "barbarians." In addition, Aquitaine retained a distinct and different military tradition and organization from the Frankish lands north of the Loire. Evidence indicates that Aquitaine remained far more influenced by Roman institutions than other parts of Gaul.[24]

However, too much may be made of this supposed separateness. The level of autonomy the Duchy of Aquitaine had is unclear. Certainly, some of the churches and monasteries that held lands in other parts of the Frankish kingdoms also had property in Aquitaine and at least one great churchman of Aquitaine, Ansoald, Bishop of Poitiers, also had land in Burgundy. In addition, a version of Latin was the common written tongue both north and south of the Loire. Through all this, Aquitaine had links to the Kingdom of the Franks through landholding, a common religion, and a common tongue, as well as common social and political structures.[25]

Provence

Eighth century Provence ran south from Lyon along the Rhone River Valley. The region was west of the Alps and east of Moorish Septimania. The area's major walled cities on the Rhone River were Arles and Avignon, while Marseilles was the region's major Mediterranean Sea port. Roman roads that ran along both sides of the Rhone connected all of these cities, and bridges at Avignon crossed the river.[26] Since the early 500s, the Franks had had an interest in Provence, fighting both Goths and Lombards to take and maintain control of the area. From the sixth to the eighth centuries, two considerations drove Frankish interests. First, maintaining the lucrative trade along the Rhone River from the Mediterranean Sea into Central Gaul, which the Franks taxed. Second, controlling the Alpine mountain passes into Northern Italy. By doing so, they controlled trade and maintained a defense against possible Lombard invasion.[27]

During the late seventh and early eighth centuries, Provence remained in the Frankish sphere of influence. However, at least some the great men of the province were decidedly anti-Charles Martel and in open conflict with him. For example, the clan headed by Duke Maurontus resisted Charles Martel's attempt to take direct control of Provence. Meanwhile, another great family headed by Patricius Abbo, supported Charles's bid to control the area.[28]

The Hammer Moves South

For Charles Martel, the victory at Tours in 732 made him the preeminent Frankish leader. This victory also made Eudo, Duke of Aquitaine, who had previously opposed Charles Martel recognize him as his overlord. In 731, Charles Martel launched two devastating raids into Aquitaine to restrain Eudo. However, Eudo's disastrous defeat at the hands of the Moors at the Battle of the River Garonne in 732 forced him to turn to his old enemy. For the time being, the arrangement between Charles Martel and Eudo secured Charles Martel's personal control of Aquitaine. The Frankish Mayor of the Palace, Charles Martel, could now turn his attention to securing southern Burgundy and Provence against the threat posed by the Muslims holding Narbonne and Nimes.[29]

Burgundy was the third Merovingian Frankish kingdom in importance after Neustria and Austrasia. With no Burgundian Mayor of the Palace, at times, the Merovingian kings directly controlled Burgundy. By the time of the Battle of Tours, some of the lords of northern Burgundy around Orleans were under Charles Martel's personal authority or closely allied with him, to the extent that he felt powerful enough to direct the area's churchmen to his satisfaction. However, the area in southern Burgundy around Lyon was not under such control. A year after defeating the Moors, Charles Martel invaded southern Burgundy and appointed his followers as judges and counts to take and enforce his mandate over the locals.[30]

In 734, Charles Martel had to put down a revolt of the Frisians that included seaborne operations in the North Sea. The year 735 saw Charles Martel back in Aquitaine. Eudo died that year and Charles Martel enforced his control over the area and over Eudo's heir, Hunoald, by occupying Hunoald's territory including many of the cities and forts. Because of this military occupation of his lands, Hunoald only ruled Aquitaine with Charles Martel's "permission." Furthermore, Charles Martel made Hunoald swear allegiance to his sons,

Carloman and Pippin.[31] Charles Martel could now move his strategic focus further south.

With affairs settled in Aquitaine, in 736 Charles Martel once more moved south, this time into the Lyonnais. His attempt to exert control over the city of Lyon and the surrounding area three years earlier produced limited success. At this time he was forced to replace many of the previously appointed officials with new men. He then led his forces down the Rhone River Valley all the way to the Mediterranean Sea. This move displaced Duke Maurontus from his position of power in the area.[32] With the Frankish military occupying the Rhone Valley, the Moors were now cut-off from easy raiding and further expansion to the east.

Maurontus made common cause with the Muslims of Narbonne to regain his previous position in Provence. He and his followers allowed the Moors into the strongly fortified city of Avignon. Maurontus then used the Moors to attack his enemies, including Charles Martel's allies. The *Annales Mettenses Priores* merely reports the city's capture by deception and the devastation of the countryside by the Moors without mentioning Maurontus's role in the action. Nonetheless, in light of other evidence, Maurontus likely had some part in the Moors' capture of the city. Other sources report that the Muslims also captured Arles.[33] The capture of Avignon and Arles was a serious strategic threat to Charles Martel's position in the Rhone Valley. It cut him off from his followers in the south, and the Alpine passes into Italy. Furthermore, the Moors could now easily attack up the river into Burgundy and east to the Alps.

The Frankish response to the capture of Avignon was massive. First, Charles Martel dispatched an advanced force under his half-brother, Duke Childebrand, which had a siege train large enough to surround the well-prepared target. Charles Martel arrived with more men and decided to take the city by assault rather than wait for it to surrender, because a second Moorish army was forming near Narbonne.[34]

The Franks had a long tradition of siege warfare. Clovis and his successors conducted sieges at Avignon in 500 and at Comminges in 585. The skills to invest and attack a city were not lost with the rise of the Mayors. Pippin the Middle conducted at least one siege at Namur in 684. The pervasiveness of fortified places throughout former Roman Gaul demanded that any effective army have the means to deal with walled cities and other kinds of fortification.[35] For their time, Frankish siege-techniques were no less effective than the Romans. The willingness of the Franks to engage in sieges indicates they were confident in their abilities.

At Avignon, the Franks used a combination of siege machines, such as battering rams and rope ladders, to assault the city. The battering rams were heavy logs with iron heads attached. They hung from a frame so that it swung back and forth to smash gates or walls. Affixed with wheels, the device sported a protective cover of woven branches, planks, layers of leather, wool, and sand to ward off stones and incendiary devices. The rope ladders were likely just knotted ropes with grappling hooks of some kind. The nature of rope ladders made their use in the attack on Avignon a commando-type or sneak attack. Furthermore, the use of rope ladders indicates that the defending force was relatively small. The attack scenario played out as follows: the Franks pushed battering rams into position against the city's gates and while the defenders rushed to fend off this attack, other Franks using rope ladders climbed over the now undefended parts of the wall. The Franks used ropes to climb not just the walls but also buildings. It is likely the suburbs had encroached on the city walls, giving the attackers platforms to help them slip over. The Franks captured the city and burned it. Even though the Franks killed and imprisoned an unknown number of enemy soldiers, insurgents forced Charles Martel and Childebrand to recapture the city the next year.[36]

After taking Avignon, he took the strategic offensive against the Moors. He "crossed the Rhone with his men and plunged into Gothic territory as far as the Narbonnaise."[37] On reaching Narbonne, Charles Martel also found an unanticipated enemy army encamped outside the city. Commanded by Yusuf Ibn Abd ar Rahman al Fihri, this new army was possibly a relief force meant for Avignon that had not had time to act before that city fell. The Franks then surrounded both the city and the army camp with a rampart and blocked river traffic into the city. Charles Martel's army also added redoubts and armed camps at intervals to combat Moorish sorties or any attempted breakouts. Furthermore, he placed catapults and batter rams in strategic locations in preparation for an assault on either the city or the camp.[38]

The Moors of Narbonne sent a dispatch to al-Andalus asking for assistance. A large relief force gathered as the great nobles and warlords in Spain gathered another army from their combined resources. Omar ibn Chaled took command of this force. Rather than cross the dangerous Pyrenees, the relief force came by sea. Ibn Chaled landed at what today is Port-Mahon where a Roman-built dock was still useable. Thinking he had achieved surprise, the Moorish general established a fortified camp on some high ground at the base of the Port-Mahon peninsula. He then moved his main force a little distance up the river and rested for the night.[39]

Charles Martel received word of Ibn Chaled's approach and countered the threat to his rear. Leaving part of his force to maintain the siege of Narbonne, Charles Martel quickly marched the rest of his army along the Via Domitia to the Valley of the River Berre. On reaching the valley, he turned and moved his force toward the sea. This blocked any Moorish attempt to reach the road. Due to good intelligence, Martel knew the location of the Moors. To rest his army, Martel had his men construct the Roman-influenced Frankish camp on the banks of the Berre in the valley of the Corbieres where an earlier Visigoth palace once stood.

The next day as the Franks approached the enemy position they deployed in their traditional infantry lines and attacked. Tradition puts The Battle of the Berre in an area between the Berre River and the marsh now called the Etang de la Palme near the village of Sigean. The location made tactical sense. The Franks secured their flanks with impassable terrain when possible. At the Battle of the Berre, they used the Berre River and the Etang de la Palme Marsh. At the Battle of Tours, they used a heavily wooded hill and the Clain River. The Moors had the sea behind them with their camp occupying the only nearby high ground. Using good tactics, the Franks cut off the Moors from their camp by a straightforward pinch from their right to their left.[40]

In their battle line, the Franks were like a living threshing machine, but instead of harvesting grain, they reaped the lives of their enemies. The Frankish infantry advanced slowly, systematically stabbing and smashing anything that stood in front of them. As was their custom, they refused to allow a gap in the line and kept moving forward. Both sides fought hard, but when the Franks killed Ibn Chaled, the Moors broke and ran. The retreating Muslims, cut off from their camp, tried to swim or take small fishing boats back to their fleet still at anchor at Port-Mahon. The Franks pursued the defeated Moors in boats, many Moors drowned as they fled. The victorious Franks now turned on the Moors' camp, which quickly surrendered. The victors captured a great amount of loot and a large number of prisoners.[41]

After his success at the Berre, Charles Martel lifted his siege of Narbonne. It is possible that his army had suffered a number of casualties in the battle at the Berre River and he did not feel strong enough to attempt a direct assault on both the city and the nearby enemy camp. Starving out either the city or the camp was a slow process and another relief force might appear at any time from Spain. Nevertheless, on his way out of Septimania, Charles Martel and his army captured the Moslem controlled cities of Agde, Beziers, and Nimes. He destroyed the cities and their suburbs.[42] This rendered those cities useless as military outposts.

Conclusion

When Charles Martel died in 741, he had not been able to capture Narbonne, but had left that to his son, Pippin, who accomplished the capture of the city in 759 after a long siege.[43] However, Charles Martel's southern strategy had largely eliminated the Moorish threat posed to the Kingdom of the Franks and, by extension, all of Christian Europe by Islamic Spain. By driving the Moors west of the Pyrenees, Charles and Pippin secured and established the southern border of what would become France. This border is still in place today.

For good or ill, Charles Martel largely established the Franks as the preeminent Christian military power in Europe. This military dominance passed to his son and his grandson Charlemagne. This power let Charles Martel's descendants build the Holy Roman Empire and sparked the Carolingian Renaissance.

Notes

1. Charles Oman, *The Dark Ages 476-918,* 4th ed. (London: Rivington, 1901), 289-291, 295-296.

2. *Annales Mettenses Priores* (The Earlier Annals of Metz) ed. B. De Simson (Hannoverae et Lipsiae: Impensis Bibliopolii Hahniani, 1905), sub anno (s. a.) 691; Bernard S. Bachrach, *Early Carolingian Warfare: Prelude to Empire* (Philadelphia: University of Pennsylvania Press, 2001), 27; Paul Fouracre, *The Age of Charles Martel* (Harlow, UK: Pearson Education Limited, 2000), 17.

3. J. M. Wallace-Hadrill, "Introduction" to *The Fourth Book of the Chronicle of Fredegar with its Continuations,* ed. and trans. J. M. Wallace-Hadill (London: Thomas Nelson and Sons, 1960), xiv-xv, xxvi-xxvii; Roger Collins, *Charlemagne* (Toronto: University of Toronto Press, Inc., 1998), 3, 6; Edward Peters "Introduction: Paul the Deacon, The Lombards, and a Sometimes Medievalist From Indiana" to Paul the Deacon's, *History of the Lombards*, trans. William D. Foulke (Philadelphia: University of Pennsylvania Press, 1974), vii; Paul Fouracre and Richard A. Gerberding, "Introduction: The Historical Context" in *Late Merovingian France: History and Hagiography*, trans and ed. (Manchester: Manchester University Press, 1996), 17.

4. Kenneth Baxter Wolf, "An Andalusian Chronicler and the Muslims" in *Conquerors and Chroniclers of Early Medieval Spain,* trans. and ed. Kenneth Baxter Wolf (Liverpool: Liverpool University Press, 1990), 29; Bruna Soravia, "Al-Maqqari" in *Medieval Islamic Civilization: an Encyclopedia*, vol. 1, ed. Josef W. Meri (New York: Routledge, 2006), 478; Konrad Hirschler, "Ibn Al -Athir, 'Ali Abu 'L hasan 'Izz Al-Din" in *Medieval Islamic Civilization: an Encyclopedia*, vol. 1, ed. Josef W. Meri (New York: Routledge, 2006), 342-343; David James, "Introduction: The History of the History" to Ibn Al-Qutiya, *Early Islamic Spain: the History of Ibn al-Qutiya*, trans. by David James (New York: Routledge, 2009), 7 -11.

5. Paul the Deacon, *History of the Lombards*, trans. William D. Foulke (Philadelphia: University of Pennsylvania Press, 1974), 6.46, note 3.

6. Collins, *Charlemagne,* 3-4; Muhammad Al-Makkari, *The History of The Mohammedan Dynasties in Spain*, vol. 1, trans. by Pascual de Gayangos (London: W. H. Allen and Co. 1843), p. 11.

7. Jordanes, *The Gothic History of Jordanes*, trans. Charles Mierow (Princeton: Princeton University Press, 1915), 191; *Annales Mettenses Priores*, s.a. 691.

8. Susan Wise Bauer, *The History of the Medieval World: From the Conversion of Constantine to the First Crusade* (New York: W. W. Norton and Co., 2010), 347; *Continuations of the Fourth Book of the Chronicle of Fredegar,* ed. and trans. J. M. Wallace-Hardill (London: Thomas Nelson and Sons,1960), 2,3,4.

9. *Les Grandes Chroniques,* trans. Robert Levine, 5.26. accessed June 27, 2014, http:// people.bu.edu/bobl/ grch4+5.htm; *Continuations of Fredegar,* 6; *Liber Historiae Francorum* (The Book of the History of the Franks: The Last Eleven Chapters) in *Late Merovingian France: History and Hagiography, 640-720,* trans and ed. Paul Fouracre and Richard A. Gerberding, (Manchester: Manchester University Press, 1996), 51-52.

10. *Continuations of Fredegar,* 10; *Annales Mettenses Priores,* s. a. 718; Fouracre, *Charles Martel,* 80.

11. Fouracre, *Charles Martel,* 17; Fouracre and. Gerberding, "Historical Context," 21-22 and 56; Bernard S. Bachrach "Was the Marchfield Part of the Frankish Constitution?" *Medieval Studies* 36 (1974): 184-185.

12. W. M. Watt and P. Cachia, *A History of Islamic Spain* (Edinburgh: Edinburgh University Press, 1965), 5.

13. Ibn Abd El-Hakem, *History of the Conquest of Spain,* trans. and ed. John Harris Jones (London: Williams & Norgate, 1858), 19; Roger Collins, *The Arab Conquest of Spain, 710-797* (Oxford: Blackwell, 1989), 36; Watt and Cachia, *History of Islamic Spain,* 8.

14. *The Chronicle of 754,* 52 and note 97; Izz al-Dīn Ibn Al-Athir, *Annales du Maghreb et de l'Espagne,* trans. E. Fagnan (Algiers: A. Jourdan, 1901), 42; *The Chronicle of Alfonso III,* in Conquerors and Chroniclers of Early Medieval Spain, trans. and ed. by Kenneth Baxter Wolf (Liverpool: Liverpool University Press, 1990), 7.

15. Al-Athir, *Annales,* 35; *Chronicle of 754,* 54, 56.

16. Muhammad Al-Makkari, *The History Of The Mohammedan Dynasties In Spain,* vol. 2, trans. by Pascual de Gayangos (London: W. H. Allen and Co. 1843), 30.

17. Collins, *Arab Conquest,* 39 and 41; "The Treaty of Tudmir (713)" in *Medieval Iberia: Readings from Christian, Muslim, and Jewish Sources,* trans. and ed. Olivia Remie Constable (Philadelphia: University of Pennsylvania Press, 1997), 37-38; *Chronicle of 754,* 87.1.

18. Andrew H. Merrills, *History and Geography in Late Antiquity* (Cambridge: Cambridge University Press, 2005), 203-204; Gregory of Tours, *A History of the Franks,* trans. Earnest Brehaut (New York: Columbia University Press, 1916) 2.37, accessed April 24, 2014, http://www.fordham.edu/ halsall/ basis/gregory-hist.asp.; Joseph F. O'Callaghan, *A History of Medieval Spain* (Ithaca, Cornell University Press, 1975), 41-42.

19. Collins, *Conquest of Spain,* 45; *The Chronicle of 754,* 62, 69.

20. William E. Watson, "The Hammer and the Crescent: Contacts between Andalusi Muslims, Franks and their Successors in Three Waves of Muslim Expansion" (PhD diss., University of Pennsylvania, 1990), 21; Al-Makkari, *Mohammedan Dynasties in Spain,* vol. 2, 38; George Childs Kohn, *Dictionary of Wars,* 3rd ed. (New York: Facts on Files, Inc., 2007), 193.

21. George T. Beech, "Aquitaine" in *Medieval France: an Encyclopedia,* ed. William W. Kibler (Philadelphia: Psychology Press, 1995), 54; Gregory, *History of the Franks,* 2.37; *Royal Frankish Annals* in *Carolingian Chronicles: Royal Frankish Annals* and *Nithard's Histories,* trans. Bernhard Walter Scholz (Ann Arbor: University of Michigan, 1970), s. a. 760 – 762, s.a. 766 – 769; Matthew Innes, Marios Costambeys and Simon MacLean, *The Carolingian World* (Cambridge: Cambridge University Press, 2011), 47.

22. Raymond Van Dam, "Merovingian Gaul and the Frankish Conquest" in *The New Cambridge Medieval History: c. 500-c. 700*, vol. 1, ed. by Paul Fouracre (Cambridge: Cambridge University Press, 2005), 203.

23. *The Fourth Book of the Chronicle of Fredegar* in *The Fourth Book of the Chronicle of Fredegar with its Continuations*, trans. and ed. by J. M. Wallace-Hardill (London: Thomas Nelson and Sons, 1960), 56, 57, 67.

24. Fouracre and Gerberding, "Historical Context", 21-23, Fouracre, *Charles Martel*, 82 – 83; *Annales Mettenses Priores*, s .a. 691, *Continuations of Fredegar*, 25.

25. Bernard S. Bachrach "Military Organization in Aquitaine Under the Early Carolingians," *Speculum* 49 (1974): 3; Yitzhak Hen, *Culture and Religion in Merovingian Gaul, A.D. 481-751* (Leiden: E. J. Brill, 1995), 6; Paul Fouracre and Richard A. Gerberding "Commentary on *Passio Leudegarii*" in *Late Merovingian France: History and Hagiography, 640-720*, ed. Paul Fouracre and Richard A. Gerberding (Manchester: Manchester University Press, 1996), 197; Hen, *Culture and Religion in Merovingian Gaul*, 25; Fouracre, *Charles Martel*, 85-86.

26. Patrick J. Geary, *Phantoms of Remembrance: Memory and Oblivion at the End of the First Millennium* (Princeton: Princeton University Press, 1994), 30; Pierre Grimal, *Roman Cities*, trans. G. Michael Woloch (Madison, WI: University of Wisconsin Press, 1983), 119-121, 188-190, 204; Raymond Chevallier, *Roman Roads*, trans. N. H. Field (Berkeley: University of California Press, 1976), 160.

27. Geary, *Phantoms of Remembrance,* 32; Gregory, *History of the Franks,* 3.6 and 3.21; Jordanes, *Gothic History,* 138; Paul, *History of the Lombards,*V.5.

28. Fouracre, *Charles Martel,* 66; Bachrach, *Early Carolingian Warfare*, 33.

29. Fouracre, *Charles Martel,* 88; Bachrach, *Early Carolingian Warfare*, 27; *Continuations of Fredegar*, 10, 13; *Chronicon Moissiacense*, (The Chronicle of Moissac) in *Monumenta Germaniae Historica: Scriptores*, vol. 1, ed. Georg Heinrich Pertz, (Hannoverae et Lipsiae: Impensis Bibliopolii Hahniani, 1826), s. a. 732, and *Chronicle of 754*, 80.

30. *Chronicle of Fredegar*, 43 and 54; *Vita Eucherii Episcopi Aurelianensi*s (The Life of Bishop Eucherius of Orleans) in *Monumenta Germaniae Historica: Scriptores rerum Merovingicarum,* vol. 7, ed. B. Krusch and W. Levison (Hannoverae et Lipsiae: Impensis Bibliopolii Hahniani, 1920), 7 - 9; *Chronicle of Fredegar,* 14.

31. *Chronicle of Fredegar*, 15 and 17; *Annales Mettenses Priores*, s .a. 735. *Vita Pardulfi Abbatis Waractensis* (The Life of Abbot Pardulf of Gueret) in *Monumenta Germaniae Historica: Scriptores rerum Merovingicarum,* Vol. 7, ed. W. Levison (Hannoverae et Lipsiae: Impensis Bibliopolii Hahniani, 1920), 21.

32. *Continuations of Fredegar,* 14, 18; Bachrach, *Early Carolingian Warfare*, 33. *Continuations of Fredegar,* 20; *Annales Mettenses Priores*, s. a. 737; Ian Wood, *The Merovingian Kingdoms*: 450-751 (London: Longman, 1994), 284; *Chronicon Moissiacense,* p 292.

34. Chronicon Moissiacense, p. 292; *Continuations of Fredegar*, 20.

35. Gregory, *History of the Franks*, 2.32, 2.33, 7.36; *Continuations of Fredegar*, 4, 11; Bernard S. Bachrach, *Merovingian Military Organization, 481-751* (Minneapolis, MN: University of Minnesota Press, 1972), 127-128; Peter Purton, *A History of the Early Medieval Siege, C.450-1200* (Woodbridge, UK: Boydell Press, 2009), 65.

36. *Continuations of Fredegar,* 20, 21; *Mappae Clavicula*, quoted in Bernard S. Bachrach's "On Roman Ramparts 300-1300" in *The Cambridge Illustrated History of Warfare: The Triumph of the West*, ed. Geoffrey Parker, (Cambridge, UK: Cambridge University Press, 2005), 73; Gregory, *History of the Franks*, 2.37; Bachrach, *Early Carolingian Warfare*, 106.

37. *Continuations of Fredegar*, 20.

38. *Continuations of Fredegar*, 20; Roger Collins, *Early Medieval Spain: Unity in Diversity, 400-1000*, 2nd ed. (New York, St. Martin's Press, 1995), 165.

39. *Continuations of Fredegar*, 20. Ibn Al-Qutiya, *Early Islamic Spain: the History of Ibn al -Qutiya*, trans. by David James (New York: Rouledge, 2009), pp. 60 -61; S. M. Imamuddin, *Muslim Spain 711-1492 A.D.: A Sociological Study* (Leiden: E .J. Brill, 1981), 63; Emile Cauvet, "Etude Historique sur L'Etablissement Des Espagnols Dans La Septimanie, Aux VIII et IX siecles et Sur La Fondation De Fontjonconse per l'Espagnol, jean au VIII siècle," *Bulletin de la Commission Archéologique de Narbonne, Tome 1* (Narbonne: Imprimerie Caillard, 1877), 367 and 370.

40. *Chronicon Moissiacense*, p. 292; *Continuations of Fredegar*, 20; Bachrach, *Early Carolingian Warfare*, 255. Paul, *History of the Lombards*, 6.54; Cauvet, "Des Espagnols Dans La Septimanie" 367-368 and 370.

41. *Annalium Fuldensium Continuatio Ratisbonensis* in *Annales Fuldenses sive Annales regni Francorum Orientalis*. ed. G.H. Pertz. (Hannoverae: Impensis Bibliopolii Hahniani, 1891), s. a. 891; *Continuations of Fredegar,* 20.

42. *Continuations of Fredegar,* 20.

43. *Continuations of Fredegar,* 24; *Chronicon Moissiacense*, s. a. 759.

Bibliography

Primary Sources

Al-Makkari, Muhammad. *The History of The Mohammedan Dynasties in Spain.*
Translated by Pascual de Gayangos, 2 vols. London: W. H. Allen and Co.
1840 - 1843.

Al-Athir, 'Izz al-Dīn Ibn, *Annales du Maghreb et de l'Espagne.* Translated by E.
Fagnan. Algiers: A. Jourdan, 1901.

Al-Qutiya, Ibn. *Early Islamic Spain: the History of Ibn al-Qutiya.* Translated by
David James. New York: Routledge, 2009.

Annales Mettenses Priores. Edited by B. De Simson. Hannoverae et Lipsiae:
Impensis Bibliopolii Hahniani, 1905.

Annalium Fuldensium Continuatio Ratisbonensis in *Annales Fuldenses sive
Annales regni Francorum Orientalis.* 107-131. Edited by G.H. Pertz.
Hannoverae: Impensis Bibliopolii Hahniani, 1891.

Chronicle of 754, The. in *Conquerors and Chroniclers of Early Medieval Spain,*
111-158.Translated and edited by Kenneth Baxter Wolf. Liverpool:
Liverpool University Press, 1990.

Chronicle of Alfonso III, The. in *Conquerors and Chroniclers of Early Medieval
Spain,* 159-177.Translated and edited by Kenneth Baxter Wolf. Liverpool:
Liverpool University Press, 1990.

Chronicon Moissiacense in *Monumenta Germaniae Historica: Scriptores:* Vol. 1,
280-313. Edited by Georg Heinrich Pertz. Hannoverae et Lipsiae:
Impensis Bibliopolii Hahniani, 1826.

El-Hakem, Ibn Abd. *History of the Conquest of Spain,* translated and edited by
John Harris Jones. London: Williams & Norgate, 1858.

Fourth Book of the Chronicle of Fredegar The, in *Fourth Book of the Chronicle of
Fredegar with its Continuations,* 1-79. Translated and edited by J. M.
Wallace-Hardill. London: Thomas Nelson and Sons, LTD., 1960.

Grandes Chroniques Les. Translated by Robert Levine. Online at http://
people.bu.edu/bobl/ _____grch4+5.htm

Gregory of Tours. *A History of the Franks.* Translated by Earnest Brehaut. New
York: Columbia University Press, 1916. Online at http://gorddcymru.org/.

Jordanes. *The Gothic History of Jordanes*. Translated by Charles Mierow.
    Princeton: Princeton University Press, 1915.

Liber Historiae Francorum (The Book of the History of the Franks: The Last
    Eleven Chapters) in *Late Merovingian France: History and
    Hagiography, 640-720*, 87-96. Translated and edited by Paul Fouracre
    and Richard A. Gerberding. Manchester: Manchester University Press,
    1996.

Mappae Clavicula quoted in Bernard S. Bachrach's "On Roman Ramparts, 300-
    1300" in *The Cambridge Illustrated History of Warfare: The Triumph of
    the West*, 64-91. Edited by Geoffrey Parker. Cambridge, UK: Cambridge
    University Press, 2005.

Paul the Deacon. *History of the Lombards*. Translated by William D. Foulke,
    Philadelphia: University of Pennsylvania Press, 1974.

Royal Frankish Annals in *Carolingian Chronicles*: *Royal Frankish Annals* and
    Nithard's Histories. Translated by Bernhard Walter Scholz. 35 -126. Ann
    Arbor: University of Michigan, 1970.

"Treaty of Tudmir, The. (713)" in *Medieval Iberia: Readings from Christian,
    Muslim, and Jewish Sources*, 37-38. Translated and edited by Olivia
    Remie Constable. Philadelphia: University of Pennsylvania Press, 1997.

Vita Eucherii Episcopi Aurelianensis in *Monumenta Germaniae Historica:
    Scriptores rerum Merovingicarum*, Vol. 7, 46-53. Edited by B. Krusch
    and W. Levison. Hannoverae et Lipsiae: Impensis Bibliopolii Hahniani,
    1920.

Vita Pardulfi Abbatis Waractensis in *Monumenta Germaniae Historica:
    Scriptores rerum Merovingicarum:* Vol. 7, 19-40. Edited by W. Levison.
    Hannoverae et Lipsiae: Impensis Bibliopolii Hahniani, 1920.

Secondary Sources

Bachrach, Bernard S. *Merovingian Military Organization, 481-751*. Minneapolis,
    MN: The University of Minnesota Press, 1972.

_____. "Military Organization in Aquitaine Under the Early Carolingians"
    Speculum 49, (1974): 1-33.

_____. "Was the Marchfield Part of the Frankish Constitution?" Medieval
    Studies 36, (1974): 178-185.

_____. *Early Carolingian Warfare: Prelude to Empire*. Philadelphia, University
    of Pennsylvania Press, 2001.

Beech, George T. "Aquitaine" in *Medieval France: an Encyclopedia*, 54-57. Edited by William W. Kibler. Philadelphia: Psychology Press, 1995.

Cauvet, Emile. "Étude Historique sur L'établissement Des Espagnols Dans La Septimanie, aux VIIIe et IX siècles et Sur La Fondation De Fontjonconse per l'espagnol, jean su VIII siècle," 343-520. *Bulletin de la Commission Archéologique de Narbonne:* Tome 1. Narbonne: Imprimerie Caillard, 1877.

Chevallier, Raymond. *Roman Roads*. Translated by N. H. Field. Berkeley: University of California Press, 1976.

Collins, Roger. *The Arab Conquest of Spain, 710-797*. Oxford: Blackwell Publishers, Ltd. 1989.

_____. *Medieval Spain: Unity in Diversity,400-1000*, 2nd edition. New York: St. Martin's Press, 1995.

_____. *Charlemagne*. Toronto: University of Toronto Press, Inc., 1998.

Fouracre, Paul and Richard A. Gerberding. "Introduction: The Historical Context" in *Late Merovingian France: History and Hagiography, 640-720*, 1-25. Translated and edited by Paul Fouracre and Richard A. Gerberding. Manchester: Manchester University Press, 1996.

_____. "Commentary on *Passio Leudegarii*" in *Late Merovingian France: History and Hagiography, 640-720*, 193 – 215. Translated and edited by Paul Fouracre and Richard A. Gerberding. Manchester: Manchester University Press, 1996.

Fouracre, Paul. *The Age of Charles Martel*. London: Longman, 2000.

Geary, Patrick J. *Phantoms of Remembrance: Memory and Oblivion at the End of the First Millennium*. Princeton: Princeton University Press, 1994.

Grimal, Pierre. *Roman Cities*. Translated by G. Michael Woloch. Madison, WI: University of Wisconsin Press, 1983.

Hen, Yitzhak. *Culture and Religion in Merovingian Gaul, A.D. 481-751*. Leiden: E. J. Brill, 1995.

Hirschler, Konrad. "Ibn Al-Athir, 'Ali Abu 'L hasan 'Izz Al-Din" in *Medieval Islamic Civilization: an Encyclopedia*, Vol. 1. Edited by Josef W. Meri, 342-343. New York: Routledge, 2006.

Imamuddin S. M. *Muslim Spain 711-1492 A.D.: A Sociological Study*. Leiden: E .J.

Brill, 1981.

Innes, Matthew, Marios Costambeys and Simon MacLean. *The Carolingian World*. Cambridge: Cambridge University Press, 2011.

James, David. "Introduction: The History of the History" to Ibn Al-Qutiya, *Early Islamic Spain: the History of Ibn al-Qutiya*. Translated by David James, 1-46. New York: Rouledge, 2009.

Kohn, George Childs. *Dictionary of Wars*, 3rd edition. New York: Facts on Files, Inc., 2007.

Merrills, Andrew H. *History and Geography in Late Antiquity*. Cambridge: Cambridge University Press, 2005.

Noble, Thomas F. X. *The Republic of St. Peter: the Birth of the Papal State, 680-825* Philadelphia: University of Pennsylvania, 1984.

O'Callaghan, Joseph F. *A History of Medieval Spain*. Ithaca, Cornell University Press, 1975.

Oman, Charles. *The Dark Ages 476-918, 4th edition*. London: Rivingtons, 1901.

Peters, Edward. "Introduction: Paul the Deacon, The Lombards, and a Sometimes Medievalist From Indiana." Introduction to Paul the Deacon. *History of the Lombards*, vii – xxi. Translated by William D. Foulke. Philadelphia: University of Pennsylvania Press, 1974.

Purton, Peter. *A History of the Early Medieval Siege,C.450-1200*. Woodbridge, UK: Boydell Press, 2009.

Soravia, Bruna. "Al-Maqqari" in Medieval Islamic Civilization: an Encyclopedia, vol. 1. Edited by Josef W. Meri, 478. New York: Routledge, 2006.

Van Dam, Raymond. "Merovingian Gaul and the Frankish Conquest" in *The New Cambridge Medieval History: c. 500-c. 700*, Volume I, 193-231. Edited by Paul Fouracre. Cambridge: Cambridge University Press, 2005.

Wallace-Hadrill, J. M. "Introduction" to *The Fourth Book of the Chronicle of Fredegar with its Continuations*. Translated and edited by J. M. Wallace-Hardill, ix-lxvii. London: Thomas Nelson and Sons,1960.

Watson, William E. "The Hammer and the Crescent: Contacts between Andalusi Muslims, Franks and their Successors in Three Waves of Muslim Expansion." PhD diss., University of Pennsylvania, 1990.

Watt, W. M. and P. Cachia. *A History of Islamic Spain*. Edinburgh: Edinburgh

University Press, 1965.

Wolf, Kenneth Baxter. "An Andalusian Chronicler and the Muslims" in *Conquerors and Chroniclers of Early Medieval Spain*. Translated and edited by Kenneth Baxter Wolf, 28-45. Liverpool: Liverpool University Press, 1990.

Wood, Ian. *The Merovingian Kingdoms, 450-751*. London: Longman, 1994.

Benjamin Church, Joseph-François Hertel, and the Origins of Irregular Warfare in the Early Colonial Period

Christopher L. Hilmer

During the French and Indian War, European-style armies fighting a conventional war played a critical role in the contest between France and Great Britain in North America. However, in the previous century a different type of fighting reigned in the primordial forests. Stealth and ambush, mobility, and lightning strikes characterized this type of warfare. The style suited the vast forested regions of northeastern America. The native peoples of the region had mastered it. In the earliest years of contact between whites and Amerindians, the natives often bested the European settlers in battle because the newcomers were generally unaccustomed to this method of fighting. Additionally, many Europeans—especially the Puritan settlers of New England—did not wish to engage in this type of warfare for cultural and religious reasons. Nonetheless, as time went on, some individuals recognized the need for the colonists to adapt and to develop military units that were capable of engaging in irregular operations. To counter threats from both Native Americans and one another, the English and the French colonists increasingly utilized guerilla warfare. Two men in particular, the Puritan Benjamin Church and the French-Canadian Joseph-François Hertel, played important roles in the development of irregular warfare amongst their respective peoples. These two men developed the tactics, advocated their usage, implemented them successfully, provided leadership in battle, and eventually laid down a mantle that was picked up by successive generations of soldiers on both sides of the nascent conflict of empires. While Church is better known today, there is no doubt that Hertel was also feared and respected. Of the two, he was likely the more experienced and proficient in irregular warfare.

Benjamin Church was born in Plymouth Colony—now Massachusetts—in 1639. His father, Richard Church, had arrived in the New World by 1630. As a skilled master carpenter, he amassed not only a fair amount of wealth, but also considerable landholdings.[1] He also amassed a large number of children, as Benjamin was the second of fifteen children born into his home. This prosperity in the early years of settlement was due, in part, to the peaceful relations which existed between the people of Plymouth Plantation and Massasoit and his people, the Wampanoag. Born into a Puritan household, hard work, strict discipline, and orthodox religion characterized Church's young life. He was, from an early age, apprenticed to his father in the carpenter's trade, evidence that he showed some aptitude for this occupation.[2] After enjoying some success in carpentry and milling, farming, and land speculation, Church married Anne Southwick in 1667. Like many others of his social standing, Church was also active in local affairs and in his church. While much of his lifestyle at this time was typical, several things marked him as different from those around him. First, while recognized as a sincere Christian he did not seem to be as doctrinaire in his religion as the majority.[3] Second, Church was far more sympathetic toward Native Americans than were most other English colonists of his day.[4] Both of these traits served him well in the coming years, and both linked to a third distinguishing trait in his life, one yet to be revealed—an aptitude for waging war.

While Church might have led a pleasant and productive life as a skilled artisan and influential leader of the colony, lasting fame came to him from his military activities, which began in King Philip's War during 1675-1676. This war, the result of decades of English encroachment on native lands and festering resentment on the part of Massasoit's son, Philip, inaugurated a military career for Church that would last for more than thirty years.[5] Church was present for the Great Swamp Fight in late 1675 during which hundreds of natives lost their lives. After an absence from the field for the birth of a child, the spring and summer of 1676 found him involved in numerous successful operations to capture and kill natives. In fact, he commanded the action that led to the death of King

Figure 1. Captain Benjamin Church (c. 1675). Artist unknown. New York Public Library - Stephen Schwarzman Building.

Philip himself. Church has been criticized by historian Guy Chet and others for winning easy victories in the latter phase of the war since the "remaining mutinous tribes were already starving, weakened, politically isolated, and on the run from the English and Indian forces."[6] On this point, Chet is correct, but it is also true that through his campaigning during King Philip's War "Church had discovered the perfect kind of military unit for dealing with the scattered remnants of the enemy—a small, cohesive, volunteer company including both Indians and English."[7] This discovery proved important for his future career.

The lessons learned and experience gained by Church and his soldiers proved useful in the numerous actions that they conducted during both King William's War (1690-1697) and Queen Anne's War (1702-1713). In these conflicts, Church fought throughout New England and in the Maritime Provinces of Canada. He utilized mixed units of colonials and natives, combining them into what were termed "ranging units,"—units noted for mobility, ambuscade, and even amphibious capabilities using whaleboats. Through his leadership, and counter to the standards of the day, Church successfully fought against Native and French enemies. In the process, he helped to create a cadre of experienced leaders and frontier soldiers who continued to utilize and improve upon his methods well after his death in 1722 at the age of seventy-eight. Church died following a fall from his horse after a visit to the home of his sick sister, an act that revealed his concern for others, and one that indicated that he remained active to the very end of his life.

Joseph-François Hertel de la Fresnière was born in the small, isolated outpost of Trois-Rivières, in the French colony of New France in 1642. Trois-Rivières was located along the Saint Lawrence River midway between the larger French centers of Québec and Montréal. The French founded the city in 1634, only a few years before Hertel's birth, and counted fewer than one hundred inhabitants at the time. While the French generally enjoyed good relations with Native Americans, their alliance with the Huron and the early and deadly encounter between Samuel de Champlain and a Mohawk war party resulted in a century long conflict between New France and the Iroquois Confederacy.[8] Trois-Rivières' proximity to the river highway of the Saint Lawrence along with its remote location made the inhabitants easy targets for the marauding bands of Iroquois who, during periods of war, sought to kill or capture anyone that they could. Although few records exist for the young Hertel, an official document of 1657 lists his occupation as a soldier. Just a few years later, in July 1661, a roving band of Iroquois captured Hertel.

The young Joseph-François, like others taken captive by the Iroquois, underwent the ritual torture that was part of warfare in their culture. Most

Europeans abhorred this torture, but some observers such as Champlain recognized that these practices were rooted in ancient religious and cultural practices and "that Indian torture was also rational and functional in a very dark way."[9] Native American historian Daniel Richter described the typical experience, stating that upon arrival in the village the captive was met by "most of the villagers holding clubs, sticks, and other weapons" from whom the captive "received heavy blows designed to inflict pain without serious injury." The captors then "stripped and led [the victim] to a raised platform in the open space inside the village, where old women led the community in further physical abuse, tearing out fingernails and poking sensitive body parts with sticks and firebrands."[10] While most prisoners would face days of horrific and painful torture, culminating in scalping and quick death by knife or hatchet, the tribe adopted some individuals as replacements for family members who were victims of war or disease. Such was the case with Hertel. In a letter written to a Catholic priest that was smuggled out of the village where he was held, he wrote "My father, I beg your blessing on the hand that writes to you, which has one of the fingers burned in the bowl of an Indian pipe, to satisfy the Majesty of God which I have offended. The thumb of the other hand is cut off; but do not tell my mother of it."[11] Hertel remained with his new family for several years until he was able to escape and eventually find his way home to his relatives who had long since given him up for dead. It is not difficult to imagine that this experience affected Hertel's life in many ways. Similarly to other Europeans captured in their youth by natives, Hertel learned their language and customs, as well as how to hunt and travel by foot, snowshoe, and canoe over long distances. He also acquired familiarity with difficult conditions and the toughness necessary for effective operations across regions of wilderness. Finally, Hertel learned first-hand the Native way of war and gained experience and insight into this style of fighting.

After his escape from the Iroquois, Hertel found himself in the middle of almost every important military operation launched by New France for the next forty years. He continued to serve in the local militia of Trois-Rivières defending the city against Iroquois attacks and he participated in both campaigns of the Carignan-Salières Regiment against the Iroquois during 1666. In 1673, Hertel accompanied Louis de Buade, Comte de Frontenac et de Palluau, the Governor General of New France on his expedition to build a fortress at Cataraqui. In 1678, he traveled north on the historic attack against the English at Hudson's Bay. While on this trip, Hertel illegally engaged in the fur trade, and upon his return, he was briefly imprisoned. This imprisonment did not last long. His capabilities and experience were too valuable to the Crown to be locked away. He continued to develop tactics and lead missions for decades. His crowning success was the raid on Salmon Falls (present day Berwick, Maine), on 27 March 1690. In this raid, the French and their native allies, members of the Wabanaki Confederacy, killed forty-three English settlers and took fifty-four prisoners. They destroyed numerous buildings and killed many cattle. Several of Hertel's sons accompanied him upon this mission, including Zacharie-François who was severely wounded during the action. Hertel was also present to help defend Québec when Sir William Phipps attacked in October of 1690. His sons carried the torch for New France during and after his lifetime, with the most famous being Jean-Baptiste Hertel de Rouville, who led the devastatingly successful raid upon Deerfield, Massachusetts in 1704. It was no idle boast when Joseph-François Hertel stated in a 1712 report that, "During all the wars no party of men or expedition has been made ready that has not included the father and some of his sons."[12] In recognition of his dedication, service, and skill he was awarded letters of nobility in 1716, becoming one of only eleven French Canadians to ever be so honored. He died on 22 May 1722 in Boucherville, Québec, at the age of eighty.

Church and Hertel transformed colonial warfare. When Europeans first came to the New World, they faced numerous disadvantages when engaging in combat with Native Americans. At the most basic level, Native Americans were hunters and warriors while "New England's defense was dependent upon farmers unaccustomed to wilderness warfare."[13] Second, while Native Americans did not possess firearms in the earliest years of conflict, they quickly acquired guns and mastered their use. One reason for their rapid adaptation to the expert use of firearms—an expertise well beyond that of the average colonist—was that the Native Americans relied more heavily upon hunting than did the European colonists, who subsisted upon livestock and crops. This helped them to develop the ability to fire accurately in a forested environment. Leadership also played a critical role and once more, there was a great gap between the battlefield leadership among natives and that of colonials. Most Native American tribes chose war chiefs through the crucible of merit and success, while for many years, colonial militia units elected leading men of the community as officers. These men often possessed no more combat experience than the men they led. It is true that at times some capable leaders emerged, but these leaders like their soldiers "were wedded to European military practices, including the use of single shot and the reliance on volleys, both ill-suited to wilderness warfare."[14] Historian Douglas Leach also observed a certain hubris on the part of colonial military men and a "lingering feeling that civilized gentlemen must not fight like savages," after which he noted that due to this feeling, "the lives of many civilized gentlemen were lost."[15] The severe losses suffered by the New England colonies in the early part of King Philip's War and those suffered by the French in their near-constant wars with the Iroquois forced both English and French to re-examine the way they were fighting, a way which seemed only to lead to defeat.

Church and Hertel were at the forefront of this transformation to a new way of waging war. While arriving at the use of similar tactics, English and French chose them for different reasons. The French had concluded, "the best way to defend New France would be to put the British colonies on the defensive, which would also neutralize their Native allies."[16] The English needed a way to blunt Native and French Canadian attacks while they carried out their larger, maritime-oriented strategy against New France. While differing in strategic intent, the tactics arrived at by both Church and Hertel were quite similar. Both men emphasized mobility and offensive action and ambush, while rejecting set piece battles and fortifications. Both men also believed that the ideal force composition included both Europeans and Native Americans. For Hertel, "Native tactics were ideally suited to North America, when allied to European discipline," providing a "marriage of military cultures" which created the "winning formula for the tactical innovations" that he advocated.[17] Similarly, Church sought "to use to advantage the best concepts of both styles of fighting," and "readily adopted Indian tactics when he realized that they were more practical than European tactics."[18] The attitudes of both men toward Native Americans and their willingness to study and adopt their fighting methods set them apart from most other military leaders of their day.

While Hertel's reputation has remained largely intact over time, the exact contributions of Benjamin Church have long been a subject of contention. Recently, scholars have questioned whether Church's innovations had any long-term ramifications, including Guy Chet, who argued against the idea of an "American way of war," by stressing instead the continuities between warfare in Europe and North America. He pointed to the final "triumph" of European-style warfare in North America and downplayed Church's influence. In his excellent book, *Conquering the American Wilderness: The Triumph of European Warfare in the Colonial Northeast,* he claimed that he set out to "find the instructional mechanism by which the knowledge acquired by Church was disseminated among colonial officers from one generation to the next."[19] According to Chet, no such mechanism existed or can be identified. He also argued that instead of adapting to changes in warfare and making improvements in methods of warfare, the quality of soldiering diminished as the colonial period moved forward. Several counter arguments can be made against these claims. First, while it is perhaps true that no formal "instructional mechanism" was ever developed, one very powerful and organic mechanism did exist for acquiring, honing, and transferring knowledge—the family structure. The significance of this mechanism for both Church and Hertel is abundantly clear. In his *The First Way of War,* historian John Grenier traces the family influence and generational experience of several groups of New England rangers noting, "The ranger companies of King William's War in fact became the nurseries for successive generations of New England rangers. By the middle of the 1740s, most New England rangers served in units under officers who had a direct connection to Church."[20] The experience of families such as the Gorhams demonstrates this point. John Gorham I was a commander for Plymouth Colony during King Philip's War, while John Gorham II "led English and Wampanoag troops during King William's War; he commanded first a company, and then, later, a battalion, and he was Benjamin Church's second-in-command during campaigns against the Abenaki."[21] Shubael Gorham, the son of John Gorham II, fought in Queen Anne's War and two of his sons, John and Joseph, fought as rangers in King George's War. In early American historian Brian Carroll's article "Savages in the Service of Empire: Native American Soldiers in Gorham's Rangers, 1744-1762," the extensive family links among Native Americans who fought alongside New England ranging units are detailed.[22]

A similar mechanism existed with the Hertel clan whose service and sacrifice for the French Crown and Canada was extraordinary. The *Dictionary of Canadian Biography* entry on Joseph-François Hertel notes that, "At one time he and seven of his sons were serving with the troops at the same time."[23] The name Hertel was as feared among the natives in Iroquoia as it was among the colonists of New England. Undoubtedly, family ties often served to produce and reinforce an esprit de corps, to gain experience at making war, and to provide a conduit for the transfer of accumulated knowledge from one generation to the next. A final item of interest is that these family ties, especially in the case of the Hertels and other French-Canadians, crossed racial and cultural lines. Like Hertel, numerous French-Canadians had passed time as captives among the Iroquois or other tribes and in some cases, bonds of kinship had been created. The Hertel family also "became involved with the nearby community of Abenakis at Odanak. In addition to negotiating issues of land use and tenancy, the Hertels and the Abenakis fought together in the intercolonial wars, beginning with the March 27, 1690 attack on Salmon Falls."[24] This alliance of families remained strong for generations. Historian Fred Anderson explained the importance of these family alliances, stating that, "a provincial army was in fact a confederation of tiny war bands, bound together less by the formal relationships of command than by an organic network of kinship and personal loyalties."[25] Finally, a common religion also helped to provide a bond between natives and Europeans. The "Praying Indians" who aided the English colonials during King Philip's War provide an example of this bond, as does the influence of Jesuit missionaries among France's Native allies. More than enough united these people, personally and professionally, to provide a means for the transfer of expertise in guerilla warfare. Nowhere was this more the case than in the irregular units commanded by men such as Church and Hertel.

Concerning Chet's second claim, that the quality of the average provincial soldier decreased as the colonial period progressed, Grenier agrees. This point has also been made concerning the French Canadian militia during the same era. Many scholars agree that the majority of soldiers in the service of both the English and French crowns saw less and less actual combat as time went on. As more men in New England and New France served in the increasingly larger armies of the later era, fewer participated in battle, much less became experienced and reliable soldiers in combat. This trend led to a greater reliance on the type of units led by men like Church and Hertel and their successors. High quality, toughness, and an ability to accomplish their missions were hallmarks of these formations. Grenier remarks that, "the Americans who most frequently experienced combat before the Seven Years' War, and thus who stamped the colonial tradition with a force disproportionate to their numbers, were the rangers."[26] Historian Jay Cassell notes a similar trend among the French Canadians stating: "The military experience of militiamen in general diminished with time. The wars with the Iroquois were effectively over in 1697. With the small number and small size of most operations against the English between 1704 and 1711, far fewer men had a chance to gain experience in combat."[27] He explained that over the next few decades a decreasing percentage of French Canadians were involved in campaigning since it was a period of relative peace, and that only a small number were ever involved in *la petite guerre*—raiding or guerilla-type warfare. Those who did see combat were generally "part of larger forces that operated along more conventional European lines" and who "served for relatively short periods of time." Cassell further states that this conclusion points to the fact that the Canadian militia possessed an elite core and that, "this core was what the Canadian high command relied on for the most important military projects. This group sustained the militia's reputation for combat effectiveness."[28] That elite core included Hertel and his men. Thus, while the overall combat effectiveness and experience of the average soldier did decrease over time, units such as those commanded by Church and Hertel continued to function at a high level and to see frequent combat because of this fact.

Church and Hertel each left a considerable legacy. While some of Church's contemporaries resented his success, he was in the eyes of many the greatest Indian fighter of his era. His early and unorthodox adoption of irregular warfare and his mastery of its practice helped to win King Philip's War. While parts of his later record were less distinguished, sometimes through no fault of his own, he nonetheless left an example of bravery, leadership, and success. He also left behind an officer corps and a body of regular soldiers who continued to serve the British Crown for many years. In recognition of his contributions to American ranging, Benjamin Church was enshrined in the U.S. Army Ranger Hall of Fame in 1992, and a gold ranger tab was affixed to his tombstone. In addition to leaving a substantial inheritance for his family, Church also left behind several histories. His memoirs, about which Douglas Leach noted that like many other great commanders in history Church not "only had great ability as a leader of men, but also a flair for the dramatic,"[29] are documents of modest historic value.

Joseph-François Hertel, nicknamed "The Hero" by his countrymen for his great service to their nation, also left a considerable legacy. About Hertel, historian Francis Parkman wrote, "To the New England of old he was the abhorred chief of Popish malignants and murdering savages. The New England of to-day will be more just to the brave defender of his country and his faith."[30] Hertel was a brave and loyal soldier and in recognition of his lengthy service on behalf of France, he was awarded letters of nobility that were passed down through his family. His legacy extended through his many sons who continued to fight for France and later for England, many of whom would earn their own honors and participate in some of the most celebrated raids of the colonial period. Hertel is recognized today as a master of guerilla warfare and one of Canada's earliest and greatest tacticians. During his lifetime, his efforts "preserved France's immense territorial acquisitions in North America and enabled a handful of French soldiers and Canadian militiamen to command respect."[31]

Two men living contemporaneously in two different cultures faced a serious and similar challenge—how to adapt to a new military environment, how to transform a military culture, and how to turn defeat on the battlefield into victory. These two great men, Benjamin Church and Joseph-François Hertel, rose to the challenge for their respective nations through innovation, the marriage of military cultures, and their own personal bravery and leadership. Each left a legacy of military professionalism and tactical success that has been recognized and emulated through the centuries and down to our own day.

Notes

1. Harold K. Woolley, "Benjamin Church and the Tactics of Wilderness Warfare" (master's thesis, Vanderbilt University, 1976), 2-3.

2. Ibid., 8-9.

3. Ibid., 5.

4. Ibid., 20-21.

5. Douglas Edward Leach, *Flintlock and Tomahawk: New England in King Philip's War* (Woodstock, VT: The Countryman Press, 2009), 14-29.

6. Guy Chet, "The Literary and Military Career of Benjamin Church: Change or Continuity in Early American Warfare," *Historical Journal of Massachusetts* 35, no. 2 (Summer 2007), 107.

7. Leach, *Flintlock and Tomahawk,* 229.

8. David Hackett Fischer, *Champlain's Dream* (New York: Simon and Schuster, 2008), 254-270.

9. Ibid., 272-273.

10. Daniel K. Richter, "War and Culture: The Iroquois Experience" *The William and Mary Quarterly,* Third Series 40, no. 4 (Oct. 1983), 286-287.

11. Letter from Hertel reproduced in Francis Parkman's, *The Old Régime in Canada: France and England in North America* (Boston: Little, Brown, and Company, 1906), 122.

12. Raymond Douville, "HERTEL DE LA FRESNIÈRE, JOSEPH-FRANÇOIS," in Dictionary of Canadian Biography, vol. 2, University of Toronto/Université Laval, 2003, accessed June 19, 2015, http://www.biographi.ca/en/bio/hertel_de_la_fresniere_joseph_francois_2E.html.

13. Eric B. Schultz and Michael J. Tougias, *King Philip's War: The History and Legacy of America's Forgotten Conflict* (Woodstock, VT: The Countryman Press, 2009), 21.

14. Ibid., 16.

15. Leach, *Flintlock and Tomahawk*, 93.

16. Colonel Horn Bernd and Dr. Roch Legault, eds., *Loyal Service: Perspectives on French-Canadian Military Leaders* (Toronto: University of Toronto Press, 2007), 37.

17. Ibid., 38.

18. Woolley, "Benjamin Church," 82.

19. Chet, "The Literary Career of Benjamin Church," 106-107.

20. John Grenier, *The First Way of War: American War Making on the Frontier* (New York: Cambridge University Press, 2005), 37.

21. Brian Carroll, "Savages in the Service of Empire: Native American Soldiers in Gorham's Rangers, 1744-1762," *The New England Quarterly* 85, no. 3 (Sept. 2012), 388.

22. Ibid.

23. Douville, "Hertel de la Fresnière," in the *Dictionary of Canadian Biography*.

24. Evan Haefeli and Kevin Sweeney, eds., *Captive Histories: English, French, and Native Narratives of the 1704 Deerfield Raid* (Amherst: University of Massachusetts Press, 2006), 37-38.

25. Fred Anderson, *A People's Army: Massachusetts Soldiers and Society in the Seven Years' War* (Chapel Hill: University of North Carolina Press, 1996), 48.

26. Grenier, *The First Way of War*, 38-39.

27. Jay Cassell, "The Militia Legend: Canadians at War, 1665-1760." Delivered at Symposium on Canadian Military History since the 17th Century, Proceedings of the Canadian Military History Conference, Ottawa, 5-9 May 2000, 63.

28. Ibid.

29. Leach, *Flintlock and Tomahawk*, 219.

30. Parkman, *The Old Régime in Canada*, 124.

31. Bernd and Legault, *Loyal Service*, 49.

Bibliography

Anderson, Fred. *A People's Army: Massachusetts Soldiers and Society in the Seven Years' War*. Chapel Hill: University of North Carolina Press, 1996.

Calloway, Colin G., ed. *Dawnland Encounters: Indians and Europeans in Northern New England*. Hanover: University Press of New England, 1991.

Carroll, Brian. "Savages in the Service of Empire: Native American Soldiers in Gorham's Rangers, 1744-1762." *The New England Quarterly* 85, no. 3 (Sept. 2012): 383-429.

Cassell, Jay. "The Militia Legend: Canadians at War, 1665-1760." Delivered at Symposium on Canadian Military History since the 17th Century, Proceedings of the Canadian Military History Conference, Ottawa, 5-9 May 2000, 59-67.

Chet, Guy. *Conquering the American Wilderness: The Triumph of European Warfare in the American Northeast*. Amherst: University of Massachusetts Press, 2003.

_____. "The Literary and Military Career of Benjamin Church: Change or Continuity in Early American Warfare." *Historical Journal of Massachusetts* 35, no. 2 (Summer 2007): 105-112.

Church, Benjamin, and Thomas Church. *The History of King Philip's War*. Boston: Howe and Norton Printers, 1825.

Douville, Raymond, "HERTEL DE LA FRESNIÈRE, JOSEPH-FRANÇOIS," in the *Dictionary of Canadian Biography*, vol. 2, University of Toronto: 2003. Accessed June 19, 2015. http://www.biographi.ca/en/bio/hertel_de_la_fresniere_joseph_francois_2E.html.

Drake, Samuel Adams. *The Border Wars of New England: Commonly called King William's and Queen Anne's Wars*. New England: Charles Scribner's Sons, 1897.

Ferling, John. "The New England Soldier: A Study in Changing Perceptions." *American Quarterly* 33, no. 1 (Spring 1981): 26-45. Accessed July 4, 2015. http://www.jstor.org/stable/2712532.

Fischer, David Hackett. *Champlain's Dream*. New York: Simon and Schuster, 2008.

Grenier, John. *The First Way of War: American War Making on the Frontier*. New York: Cambridge University Press, 2005.

Haefeli, Evan and Kevin Sweeney, eds. *Captive Histories: English, French, and Native Narratives of the 1704 Deerfield Raid.* Amherst: University of Massachusetts Press, 2006.

Hirsch, Adam J. "The Collision of Military Cultures in Seventeenth-Century New England." *The Journal of American History* 74, no. 4 (March 1988): 1187 -1212. Accessed May 19, 2015. http://www.jstor.org/stable/1894407.

Horn, Colonel Bernd and Dr. Roch Legault, eds. *Loyal Service: Perspectives on French-Canadian Military Leaders.* Toronto: University of Toronto Press, 2007.

Leach, Douglas Edward. *Flintlock and Tomahawk: New England in King Philip's War.* Woodstock, VT: The Countryman Press, 2009.

Malone, Patrick M. *The Skulking Way of War: Technology and Tactics among the New England Indians.* Plymouth, MA: Plymouth Plantation, 1991.

Merrell, James H. "Second Thoughts on Colonial Historians and American Indians." *The William and Mary Quarterly* 69, no. 3 (July 2012): 451- 512. Accessed April 9, 2015. http://www.jstor.org/stable/10.5309/ willmaryquar.69.3.0451.

Parkman, Francis. *The Old Régime in Canada: France and England in North America, Vol. 1.* Boston: Little, Brown, and Company, 1906.

Radisson, Pierre-Esprit. *Les Aventures Extraordinaires d'un Coureur des Bois.* Québec: Nota Bene, Inc., 1999.

Richter, Daniel K. "War and Culture: The Iroquois Experience." *The William and Mary Quarterly*, Third Series, 40, no. 4 (Oct. 1983): 528-559. Accessed May 15, 2015. http://www.jstor.org/stable/1921807.

Schultz, Eric B., and Michael J. Tougias. *King Philip's War: The History and Legacy of America's Forgotten Conflict.* Woodstock, VT: The Countryman Press, 2009.

Steele, Ian K. *Warpaths: Invasions of North America.* Oxford: Oxford University Press, 1994.

Waldman, Carl. *Atlas of the North American Indian.* New York: Facts on File, 2009.

Woolley, Harold K. "Benjamin Church and the Tactics of Wilderness Warfare." Unpublished master's thesis, Vanderbilt University, 1976.

The Impact of Cars on Cities

Christopher N. Schloemer

Americans love their cars. By the end of the twentieth century, America had become a "car-crazy country" in which the automobile was indispensable.[1] However, the proliferation of automobiles and the mobility it gave the average American had a great impact on the development of America's cities. The automobile rose through the conflict of competing for dominance of the city streets, changing the nature of the city street, and in turn changing the landscape of the American city—not always for the better. Increased automobile usage required changes to accommodate parking and impacted the environment. Increased mobility caused urban sprawl, exacerbated by the urban and interstate highway systems that led to the meteoric rise of the suburb, decimating urban population centers and the urban economy. Urban highways and the Interstate Highway System, although developed to help cities, actually hurt them.

Automobiles began as an oddity but quickly grew to dominate American transportation in the twentieth century. Even before 1900, Henry Ford began laying the foundation for mass production of automobiles. Mass production resulted in automobiles that were affordable. The automobile industry grew greatly during the early years of the century. The number of registered automobiles rose from 8,000 in 1900 to 458,000 by 1910. Employment in automobile factories was less than 10,000 in 1900, but rose to 37,000 in 1910 and over 200,000 in 1920. As automobiles became more and more popular, most Americans seemed to find them indispensable. By 1939, there were over 23 million automobiles registered in the United States. Production rose to over four million per year in the early 1940s. After World War II, production increased to over five million cars and one million other vehicles. By 1960, registrations had risen to 82 million. In 1980, the number of automobile registrations rose to 156 million and by 2000, there were 221 million. By the end of the century, 89 percent of Americans aged 16 and over were licensed drivers; of America's 107 million households, more than 85 million owned one or more cars or trucks.[2] This explosion in the number of automobiles on the road greatly impacted the nature of the city in the early twentieth century. First, the automobile reshaped the landscape of the city, beginning with the city street.

Automobiles soon changed the usage of the city street. As automobiles vied for space in the city, they competed with other traditional users of the city streets. Society had to decide on the role of the city street and who had the right of way. At the turn of the century, according to Peter D. Norton, in his article "Street Rivals: Jaywalking and the Invention of the Motor Age Street,"

> Streets were shared by several sociotechnical systems. Private, horse-drawn vehicles and city services (such as streetcars, telephones, and water supply) depended upon them. Pedestrians, pushcart vendors, and children at play used them as well. The balance was always delicate and sometimes unstable, and crowds of automobiles soon disrupted it.[3]

Streets had long been used in many different ways. Pedestrians, vendors, horses-drawn vehicles, children at play, and others all shared the crowded city streets. Streets were thoroughfares for all. Cars had no right of way over these other users. This controversy was not solved easily.

Although automobile traffic increased rapidly in the first two decades of the twentieth century, the question of who owned the city street was still unanswered. The rivalry between cars and pedestrians was the most heated. Pedestrians forced from the street by automobiles blamed the problem on "joy riders," and irritated drivers referred to pedestrians as "jaywalkers."[4] This battle

Figure 1 A panoramic image capturing the corner of 5th and Spring Streets captured by C. C. Pierce & Co., Los Angeles. C. 1910

continued for the next decade, but by 1930, "in the new street equilibrium based on automobile supremacy . . . most agreed, readily or grudgingly, that streets were chiefly motor thoroughfares, open to others only under carefully defined restrictions."[5] Pressured by new traffic regulations and safety measures, pedestrians "relinquished the streets."[6] Once this social reconstruction of the city street occurred, cities needed to be physically reconstructed. For example, city planners needed to figure out where to put all of these vehicles.

One way that automobiles changed the landscape of cities was in the need for parking. In the first two decades of the twentieth century, curb parking was the norm. As the number of cars increased, not all could be curb parked and this caused a traffic control problem. The American Community Survey estimated that in 2009, over 95 percent of American workers drove private automobiles to work.[7] Employees had to keep their cars somewhere while they were at work and curbs would not suffice to solve the problem. Automobiles are parked 95 percent of the time, so parking became a burning question for most Americans; "parking, like driving, has been a fundamental part of our everyday life since the invention of the automobile."[8] The cities had to deal with this. As a result of these changes, parking lots now take up over one-third of all land area in some U.S. cities. This has had a great impact on cities. These large, impervious surfaces increase runoff, impact watersheds, and increase heat; most are considered a necessary evil.[9] The increase in automobiles in the city resulted in other physical changes as well. The term "urban sprawl" reflects another major change in cities brought about by the proliferation of automobiles.

As more and more Americans owned automobiles, they gradually discovered that they had the ability to spread out. This resulted in urban sprawl, characterized by the population moving outwards from the city centers. One definition of sprawl is "a process of large-scale real estate development resulting in low-density, scattered, discontinuous car-dependent construction, usually on the peripheral of declining older suburbs and shrinking city centers."[10] One historian stated, "[The] effect of the auto on the city is analogous to what astronomers call the big bang theory of the universe. . . . In the past, cities sucked inward. With the car, they exploded outward."[11] In droves people moved out of the cities and into the suburbs.

Originally, only the wealthy and powerful lived in the suburbs. However, by the 1920s, "it had become a mass movement."[12] Many working-class and middle -class families discovered they could only afford homes far from the city, as the land prices were lower. After World War II, the Veterans Administration and the Federal Housing Administration offered affordable loans that helped more

Americans buy a home. This promoted home ownership. Because of their rigid eligibility standards, these loans favored standardized subdivision designs, which burgeoning suburbs accommodated in the construction of new subdivisions.[13] Established centers, mixed-use neighborhoods, and narrow, versatile streets characterized traditional cities, which provided pedestrians with most necessary services within the range of a five-minute walk.[14] People now lived in suburban communities that did not contain mixed-use areas. There were residential areas, work areas, and shopping centers. All were separated; people could not walk to get what they needed. This perpetuated the need for cars. The working-class and middle-class families in the suburbs became more and more dependent upon cars to transport themselves. Demand increased, and automobiles became more readily available.

Cars had become more affordable. By 2001, 86 percent of low-income households in America owned at least one car.[15] Cities spread out. While most cities of the early twentieth century covered about one hundred square miles, "the new city routinely encompasses two to three thousand [square] miles."[16] For example, "from 1970 to 1990, the population of metropolitan Los Angeles grew by 45 percent, but the land area of the Los Angeles metropolis sprawled by a whopping 300 percent beyond its former size."[17] However, early in the twentieth century, moves to the suburbs were not considered a problem.

The spread of population to suburbia seemed to be a good thing to most Americans as they chased the American dream. At the First National Conference on City Planning in 1909, "suburbanization was seen at the time not as a problem, but as a strategy for allowing people in congested cities to escape to areas where they could enjoy higher quality housing, healthier lifestyles, and parks and open space."[18] Still, most Americans felt that the cities were still important, that "a prosperous downtown was as vital to the well-being of a city as a strong heart was to the well-being of a person."[19] Early planners wanted to incorporate transportation systems in a coordinated effort to help both people and cities. The explosion of mass-produced automobiles complicated these goals. Traffic laws and traffic control measures were swamped by the massive introduction of cars into the system. Because of their "love affair" with automobiles, Americans rebuilt their cities.[20] City planners decided that urban freeways would be the answer. They believed that easier access to city centers through freeways would help cities by easing access. "They saw roads, transit, and freeways as potential tools for urban renewal, particularly to revive flagging central business districts."[21] However, these freeways further changed the face of the city and encouraged urban sprawl.

Transportation shaped cities. How people got around determined how they lived; transportation "determines the form of our places."[22] Urban highways did this to the cities. The head of the Bureau of Public Roads at the time, Thomas H. McDonald, thought that a system of interregional highways "could ensure that historic centers of population would remain the centers of their metropolitan regions" and would "bring in people more conveniently."[23] He also proposed circumferential highways (ring roads or beltways) to "allow trucks to bypass the urban core, relieving unnecessary congestion . . . in reality the system turned America's cities inside out."[24] Urban highways "invited more traffic, increased congestion, lengthened commutes, guaranteed the sprawl of a region far beyond the needs of its growing population."[25] Much of this resulted from problems with planning.

Although early planners tried to plan for automobiles using a "holistic vision of transportation planning that recognized its symbiotic interaction with land use," the results were far from this vision.[26] The reality was that these holistic plans were expensive, difficult to implement, and politically sensitive. Unfortunately, "politically expedient decisions about public finance have had unanticipated, but profound and long lasting effects on projects, travel and urban form."[27] When the urban freeways were eventually built, they did not follow the lines that early planners had anticipated. This was due to money and politics and it caused more problems than it resolved.[28] These factors greatly impacted cities.

Finance and politics changed the way urban freeways were planned in the 1930s. American planners realized that they needed to redesign cities as they had not been built to accommodate cars. Many of America's registered drivers lived, or at least worked, in urban areas and it was obvious change was necessary. However, the depression, and the resulting dropping property tax revenues, impacted the money that cities had to improve their street systems and local freeways. Nevertheless, automobile ownership and use continued to rise in the 1930s. To resolve this, funding began to come from state and government gas taxes. This shifted the control of developing urban highways from local leaders to federal and state officials, who had a different outlook and priorities when it came to highway development; they were more interested in rural development, for example, farm-to-market transportation, than they were in urban freeways. These officials were also more interested in a technical, traffic-focused vision that minimized costs rather than urban planning.[29] Planners did try to redesign cities, but "instead of designing a transportation system to get the most out of America's cities, America redesigned its cities to get the most out of the automobile."[30] Engineers built urban highways, "designed for automotive speeds and the nearly exclusive use of motorists."[31] The engineering vision that satisfied financial and political concerns ended up overriding the need for careful urban planning and benefitted rural areas to the detriment of cities. This just made it easier to live in the suburbs, exacerbating urban sprawl and greatly impacting city economies.

Urban sprawl had a devastating effect on city economies. Large industrial cities struggled as they lost "staggering numbers of industrial jobs as manufacturing companies . . . either closed their doors, moved operations to the suburbs, or departed the metropolitan area altogether."[32] In the 1940s, the move to the suburbs was already "draining cities of industry, population, and retail trade."[33] Instead of living in the cities, people wanted to live in the suburbs, causing the population of the city to "decant slowly into the countryside."[34] Automobiles allowed people to escape "urban ills" such as "crime, race, and the declining quality of public services, particularly education."[35] As population movement occurred and people vacated cities, property wasted away in the urban core, resulting in unused lots, high vacancies, low rents, and deteriorating values.[36] However, the suburbs thrived.

Shopping followed the movement of the population, leaving the urban core for outlying areas. When retailers realized that automobiles enabled shoppers to come to them, "completely independent from the place where people lived, new centers for shopping could go almost any place where roads brought people over inexpensive real estate."[37] Retailers began to take advantage of the chain establishment concept.

> From fast food to gasoline to motel rooms, regardless of the product, the marketing was the same. Familiar roadside architecture—cheap to build, easy to replicate, and easy to recognize from behind the wheel of a moving vehicle—catered to the mobile American, who demanded predictability in unfamiliar places.[38]

Downtown department stores and smaller retailers followed the crowd out of the city. This led to the disintegration of city community centers and the loss of jobs.

As people discovered they could live outside of the city, urban sprawl resulted in the loss of jobs in the city, and an increase in suburban jobs that also encouraged people to move to the suburbs. From 1973-1975, America lost five million blue-collar jobs but gained from 82 to 110 million jobs in the service industry.[39] Fewer people commuted into the city as stores and businesses moved to the suburbs, and they were able to find service jobs outside the city. The suburbs became independent of the urban centers and became like independent cities. They became the preferred place to not only live, but also work, leaving little need to travel into the city. "The Suburb now dominates. It is where most people live and work. And so it has switched places with the urban environment, and the roles they serve have also reversed. It is the suburbs that are now the centers of commerce, industry, and business."[40] Urban sprawl was also accelerated by the development of the Interstate Highway System.

America's system of interstate highways has brought tremendous positive results. However, the benefits of the Interstate Highway System came at a great cost to cities and their residents.[41] The interstate system increased mobility, productivity, and prosperity. In a 1956 article in *The Saturday Evening Post,* Richard Thruelsen lauded the Federal-Aid Highway Act of 1956, which represented "one of the most astounding pieces of legislation in history . . . such a monumental conception of national public works that its accomplishment will literally dwarf any previous work of man."[42] He spoke about how the "urban expressways" would "completely change the traffic pattern (and in many ways the growth pattern) of the city."[43] Thruelsen was correct in this regard. He also stated that they were called freeways because of the free movement of traffic that would result; commuters could bisect the city and get from the center to the outer belt with "a few minutes of easy driving," and that the projects would "profit every section of the urban community."[44] The end result did not confirm this statement. In fact, some communities were destroyed.

The interstate system did change the pattern of the American city. The fact that the federal government was paying ninety percent of the costs for these highways had "state and city officials clamoring for the easy money, regardless of their traffic needs."[45] Highway engineers tended to study traffic trends and build highways where they thought the traffic would be the worst instead of studying the urban region itself. These highways often divided neighborhoods, especially low-income neighborhoods, while wealthier neighborhoods got preferential treatment or were able to stop proposed projects altogether.[46] Not only neighborhoods, but parks, historic districts, and environmentally sensitive areas were demolished to make space for the highways.[47] In the words of one critic, "The desire of the car owner to take his car wherever he went no matter what the social cost drove the Interstate Highway System, with all the force and lethal effect of a dagger, into the heart of the American City."[48] Robert Moses, head of the New York's slum clearance committee, controlled the largest public works projects in America from 1924 to 1968.[49] He is estimated at having evicted up to a quarter million people and destroyed many communities and historic sections of the city to construct hundreds of miles of parkways and highways.[50] By 1966, "of all the historical landmarks of local identity recorded in detail over the previous three decades by the National Park Service's Historical American Buildings survey, nearly half had been demolished or mutilated beyond recognition."[51] One critic said that "the time is approaching in many cities when there will be every facility for moving about the city and no possible reason for going there."[52] Not until the mid-1960s did engineers begin to take the protection of social and environmental values into consideration.[53] By then, the cities had changed astronomically.

Historians have had many views on the impact of the car on the city. A focus on the issue of urban sprawl seems to be the most common lament about the automobile's negative impact, especially in the past few decades. In a quick search for books on urban sprawl in the San Antonio Public Library database, twenty-one books came up, ranging in publication date from 1993 to 2013. In addition to the authors cited in previous paragraphs, many others decry urban sprawl and advocate rebuilding cities without the automobile as a primary focus. For example, Taras Grescos, in his book *Straphanger: Saving Our Cities and Ourselves from the Automobile,* says automobiles cause "never ending metropolitan sprawl, high carbon emissions, and global gridlock."[54] He points out that the majority of the world's population does without cars, even in large cities. "Half the population of New York, Toronto, and London do not own cars . . . done right, public transport can be faster, more comfortable, and cheaper than the private automobile."[55] Jeff Speck, in his book *Walkable City: How Downtown Can Save America One Step at a Time,* states that due to the "sheer waste of suburban sprawl" and its propensity to make cars indispensable, "the inactivity-inducing convenience, often violent speed, and toxic exhaust of our cars" make it more likely that youth will live shorter lives than their parents.[56] Speck postulates that planning for cities with a focus on walking, rather than driving, will enhance "wealth, health, and sustainability."[57] The examples are endless, but solutions to urban sprawl will be difficult.

The rise of the automobile greatly impacted cities during the twentieth century. Cars reshaped city landscapes, changed city residential patterns, and impacted city economies. The popularity of automobiles grew quickly, changing the nature of the city street in America from being pedestrian-dominated to being ruled by the automobile. Americans' dependence on the car required parking, which also changed the landscape of the city, and caused damage to the environment. Automobile traffic also created pollution issues. Urban sprawl changed the nature of the city as people, businesses, and jobs moved from the cities to the suburbs, devastating city economies. Urban highways and the national Interstate Highway System, instead of helping the city, only exacerbated the problems. The rise of suburbia became part of the American dream, but it contributed to the demise of the city. Automobile development had a huge impact on the development of the American city, and American society in general. By studying the history of this impact, Americans can learn to not repeat mistakes and to instead create a vibrant, clean urban structure that will improve city life.

Notes

1. James T. Patterson, *Restless Giant: The United States from Watergate to Bush V. Gore* (New York: Oxford University Press, 2005), 5.

2. John Milton Cooper, Jr., *Pivotal Decades: the United States, 1900-1920* (New York: W. W. Norton & Company, 1990), 13, 133-134; Ben Joseph Eran, *Rethinking a Lot: the Design and Culture of Parking* (Cambridge MA: The MIT Press, 2012), 62; John B. Rae, *The American Automobile: A Brief History* (Chicago: University of Chicago Press, 1965), 145, 176, 223; Patterson, *Restless Giant: The United States from Watergate to Bush V. Gore*, 38, 357.

3. Peter D. Norton, "Street Rivals: Jaywalking and the Invention of the Motor Age Street," *Technology and Culture* (April 2007): 332.

4. Ibid.

5. Ibid., 332-333.

6. Ibid., 334.

7. Eran, *Rethinking a Lot: the Design and Culture of Parking,* 13.

8. Ibid., 3.

9. Ibid., ix.

10. Dolores Hayden, *A Field Guide to Sprawl* (New York: W. W. Norton & Company, 2004), 8.

11. Alex Marshall, *How Cities Work: Suburbs, Sprawl, and the Roads Not Taken* (Austin: The University of Texas Press, 1959), 44.

12. Robert Bruegmann, *Sprawl: A Compact History* (Chicago: University of Chicago Press, 2005), 33.

13. Richard Moe and Carter Wilkie, *Changing Places: Rebuilding Community in the Age of Sprawl* (New York: Henry Holt and Co. 1997), 49.

14. Anders Duany, Elizabeth Plater-Zyberk, and Jeff Speck, *Suburban Nation: The Rise of Sprawl and the Decline of the American Dream* (New York: North Point Press, 2000), 15-16.

15. Brian D. Taylor, "Putting a Price on Mobility: Cars and Contradictions in Planning," *Journal of the American Planning Association* 72, no. 3 (Summer 2006): 279-284.

16. Marshall, *How Cities Work: Suburbs, Sprawl, and the Roads Not Taken,* 44.

17. Moe and Wilkie, *Changing Places: Rebuilding Community in the Age of Sprawl,* 69.

18. Jeffrey R. Brown, Eric A. Morris, and Brian D. Taylor, "Planning for Cars in Cities: Planners, Engineers, and Freeways in the 20th Century," *Journal of the American Planning Association* 75, no. 2 (Spring 2009): 162.

19. Richard E. Foglesong, *Downtown: Its Rise and Fall, 1880-1950* (New Haven CT: Yale University Press, 2003).

20. Brown, Morris, and Taylor, "Planning for Cars in Cities: Planners, Engineers, and Freeways in the 20th Century,"162.

21. Ibid., 167.

22. Marshall, *How Cities Work: Suburbs, Sprawl, and the Roads Not Taken,* 44.

23. Brown, Morris, and Taylor, "Planning for Cars in Cities: Planners, Engineers, and Freeways in the 20th Century," 162.

24. Ibid.

25. Moe and Wilkie, *Changing Places: Rebuilding Community in the Age of Sprawl,* 61.

26. Brown, Morris, and Taylor, "Planning for Cars in Cities: Planners, Engineers, and Freeways in the 20th Century,"162.

27. Ibid., 161.

28. Ibid., 161, 168.

29. Ibid., 168, 170.

30. Moe and Wilkie, *Changing Places: Rebuilding Community in the Age of Sprawl,* 59.

31. Norton, "Street Rivals: Jaywalking and the Invention of the Motor Age Street." 333.

32. Bruegmann, *Sprawl: A Compact History,* 46.

33. Moe and Wilkie, *Changing Places: Rebuilding Community in the Age of Sprawl,* 60.

34. Ibid.

35. Ibid., xi.

36. Ibid.

37. Ibid., 65.

38. Ibid.

39. Ibid., 69.

40. Marshall, *How Cities Work: Suburbs, Sprawl, and the Roads Not Taken,* xv.

41. Brown, Morris, and Taylor, "Planning for Cars in Cities: Planners, Engineers, and Freeways in the 20th Century,"162.

42. Thruelsen, Richard, "Coast to Coast Without a Stoplight: Our Amazing New Federal Highway Program Promises 41,000 Miles of Billboard-Free, Possible Toll-Free, Superroads. And it Will Cost Fifty Billion Dollars," *The Saturday Evening Post* (October 20, 1956): 23.

43. Ibid., 54.

44. Ibid.

45. Moe and Wilkie, *Changing Places: Rebuilding Community in the Age of Sprawl,* 62.

46. Brown, Morris, and Taylor, "Planning for Cars in Cities: Planners, Engineers, and Freeways in the 20th Century." 172.

47. Raymond A. Mohl, "The Interstates and the Cities: The U.S. Department of Transportation and the Freeway Revolt, 1966-1973," *The Journal of Political History* 20, no. 2 (2008), 193.

48. Ibid.

49. Moe and Wilkie, *Changing Places: Rebuilding Community in the Age of Sprawl,* 61.

50. Ibid.

51. Ibid., 66.

52. Ibid., 63.

53. Ibid.

54. Taras Grescoe, *Strap Hanger: Saving Our Cities and Ourselves from the Automobile* (New York: Henry Holt and Company, LLC, 2012), 14-15.

55. Ibid., 39.

56. Jeff Speck, *Walkable City: How Downtown Can Save America, One Step at a Time.* (New York: Farrar, Straus and Giroux, 2012), 1.

57. Ibid., 16.

Bibliography

Brown, Jeffrey R., Eric A. Morris, and Brian D. Taylor. "Planning for Cars in Cities: Planners, Engineers, and Freeways in the 20th Century." *Journal of the American Planning Association* 75, no. 2 (2009): 161-177.

Bruegmann, Robert. *Sprawl: A Compact History.* Chicago: University of Chicago Press, 2005.

Cooper, John Milton Jr. *Pivotal Decades: the United States, 1900-1920.* New York: W. W. Norton & Company, 1990.

Duany, Anders, Elizabeth Plater-Zyberk, and Jeff Speck. *Suburban Nation: The Rise of Sprawl and the Decline of the American Dream.* New York: North Point Press, 2000.

Eran, Ben Joseph. *Rethinking a Lot: the Design and Culture of Parking.* Cambridge MA: The MIT Press, 2012.

Foglesong, Richard E. *Downtown: Its Rise and Fall, 1880-1950.* New Haven CT: Yale University Press, 2003.

Grescoe, Taras. *Strap Hanger: Saving Our Cities and Ourselves from the Automobile.* New York: Henry Holt and Company, LLC, 2012.

Hayden, Dolores. *A Field Guide to Sprawl.* New York: W. W. Norton & Company, 2004.

Marshall, Alex. *How Cities Work: Suburbs, Sprawl, and the Roads Not Taken.* Austin: The University of Texas Press, 1959.

Moe, Richard, and Carter Wilkie. *Changing Places: Rebuilding Community in the Age of Sprawl.* New York: Henry Holt and Co., 1997.

Mohl, Raymond A. "The Interstates and the Cities: The U.S. Department of Transportation and the Freeway Revolt, 1966-1973." *The Journal of Political History* 20, no. 2 (2008): 193-226.

Norton, Peter D. "Street Rivals: Jaywalking and the Invention of the Motor Age Street." *Technology and Culture* (2007): 331-359.

Patterson, James T. *Restless Giant: The United States from Watergate to Bush V. Gore.* New York: Oxford University Press, 2005.

Perez, Laura, Fred Lurmann, John Wilson, Manuel Pastor, Sylvia J. Brandt, Nino Kunzil, and Rob McConnell. "Near-Roadway Pollution and Childhood Asthma: Implications for Developing "Win-Win" Compact Urban

Development and Clean Vehicle Strategies." *Environmental Health Perspectives* (2012): 1619-1626.

Rae, John B. *The American Automobile: A Brief History.* Chicago: University of Chicago Press, 1965.

Speck, Jeff. *Walkable City: How Downtown Can Save America, One Step at a Time.* New York: Farrar, Straus and Giroux, 2012.

Taylor, Brian D. "Putting a Price on Mobility: Cars and Contradictions in Planning." *Journal of the American Planning Association* 72, no. 3 (2006): 279-284.

Thruelsen, Richard. "Coast to Coast Without a Stoplight: Our Amazing New Federal Highway Program Promises 41,000 Miles of Billboard-Free, Possible Toll-Free, Superroads. And it Will Cost Fifty Billion Dollars." *The Saturday Evening Post* (October 20, 1956): 23-24, 54, 59, 61, 64-65.

The Zulu Identity: Surviving Colonialism, Apartheid, and King Shaka

Jessica R. Orr Flinchum

> There is no clear evidence of when anybody first came to think of themselves as 'Zulu.' Even when people do eventually record themselves as 'Zulu', it remains slippery, changeable, one of several possible simultaneous identities.
>
> —Dan Wylie, *Myth of Iron: Shaka in History*

The Zulu kingdom is now KwaZulu, one of nine South African provinces. It is situated on South Africa's eastern coast along the Indian Ocean and encompasses only 7.7 percent of the country's total area.[1] Although KwaZulu now has eleven official languages, including English and Xhosa, Zulu dominates as the primary spoken language of 80.9 percent of KwaZulu's population.[2] In the 1990s, approximately eight million people living in cities of suburban South Africa (outside the coastal borders of KwaZulu) considered themselves Zulu or members of interrelated ethnic groups.[3] This identity persists in spite of apartheid efforts that lasted until the late twentieth century to eliminate ethnic and linguistic distinctions by grouping all blacks together and attempts to oust them from South Africa en masse.[4] This *Zulu identity* originated from the heroification of King Shaka kaSenzangakhona (r. 1816 – 1828). It can be examined in two parts: the popular acknowledgment paid to Shaka's sweeping social, political, and military reforms, including the socio-militaristic regimentalization of all aspects of Zulu life; and the more recent role of dehumanization as employed by European colonialists and later apartheidists, together with the African cultural response.

Shaka's Early History

Written history of the Zulu Kingdom typically begins with a non-Zulu: Chief Dingiswayo (r. 1808 – 1818) of the Mthethwa, a Nguni-speaking group of the Bantu population in South Africa. Dingiswayo distinguished himself among the myriad of chiefs and war-makers in South African history as a political and military reformer whose conquests were driven mainly by "his desire to end the internecine fighting between different communities and to bring them under a single government."[5] Dingiswayo's legacy lies not in his own accomplishments, however, but in those of his protégé, an unwanted bastard child named Shaka. During Dingiswayo's time, the neighboring Zulu comprised a small lineage of approximately two thousand people. The indulgence of their chief Senzangakhona kaJama in a scandalous liaison with a Qwabe princess, although eventually legitimized through marriage, was at best taboo[6] and at worst considered incestuous.[7] The result of their liaison, Shaka (a name which actually refers to a gastrological malady), grew up unwanted and ridiculed, the perfect underdog for any story. As a teenager, he took refuge among the Mthethwa, joined their army, and rose through the ranks to military prominence.[8]

Dingiswayo became this young warrior savant's mentor. In many ways, Dingiswayo's social appeal was appropriate for a young Zulu, whose people have been described by South African academic Dan Wylie as having "wanted to belong, to be rooted, to feel naturalized . . . at least some of the Zulu were extraordinarily sensitive about the question of their origins."[9] The scandalous tragedy of Shaka's origin plays naturally into that attitude and provides a colorful basis for South African identity. African politicians would later draw upon the name and house of Shaka to define and legitimize future sociopolitical and economic struggles.[10]

Military and Social Reform

When the Zulu chief died, Shaka returned to the tribe of his birth and seized power over the Zulu community, adapting many of Dingiswayo's policies and approaches, though not necessarily his sociopolitical aspirations. Dingiswayo's chief contribution to Shaka's legacy was the reorganization of his military from fighting units based on lineage into integrated, age-based regiments, thereby weakening the influence of territorially-based familial associations.[11] Shaka would run with this motif by dividing his own army into four regiments primarily based on age and marital status.[12] This regimentalization separated young men from the middle-aged and the elderly, which in turn unified ranks previously ruled by generational tensions. In their article on "Zulu Masculinities, Warrior Culture and Stick Fighting: Reassessing Male Violence and Virtue in South Africa" for the *Journal of Southern African Studies*, Dr. Benedict Carton and Dr. Robert Morrell emphasized the Zulu attribute of respect (*inhlonipho*) as a necessary balancing agent in masculine interactions by requiring "youths [honor their] elders through uncompromising practices of social avoidance, making vigilant restraint a vital part of their advance to adulthood."[13] In other words, *inhlonipho* constrained the social behavior and upward mobility of assertive young men—no doubt as Shaka also experienced during his youth. Age-based regiments effectively neutralized such restraints.

Most historical accounts hail Shaka as a military genius. Besides the regimental system, he also modified the Zulu's primary warfighting technique by adapting their fighting spear, *assegai*, into the *iklwa*, now a heavy broad-bladed weapon with a shortened haft, as well as converting the shield into an offensive weapon.[14] However, Wylie alleges that Shaka's cousin was actually the true creator of the short-hafted stabbing spear,[15] and that the only truly original military tactic that Shaka introduced into Zulu warfare was the *kisi*, essentially a simple challenge-and-password system.[16] There is some merit to that critique; the bulk of Shaka's major innovations were actually modifications of preexisting tactics and policies. However, it would be overly simplistic to use pure innovation as the only yardstick for measuring military genius. Dingiswayo also changed the political structure by centralizing power across his territory, and leaving intact chiefdoms which willingly submitted to his power and offered tribute rather than continued resistance.[17] This, too, was a post-conquest policy that Shaka adapted and maintained, though with far less benevolence than his mentor. Foreign affairs columnist and former CIA officer Donald R. Morris summarized Shaka's bloodthirsty adaptation as such:

> Where Dingiswayo saw combat as an unfortunate but inevitable necessity when palaver had failed, Shaka saw it as the one safe and sure method of political growth. Dingiswayo would at once accept submission and chain the dogs of war, but Shaka saw that an undefeated clan, temporarily left in peace, was always free to turn on a paramount chieftain in a more propitious season. [Shaka's regiment] had more than once been sent to deal with a clan they had already vanquished, and Shaka preferred to smash such a clan the first time, incorporating the fragments into an organization of his own making. . . . He despised a show of force designed merely to convince an enemy that resistance was useless.[18]

Terror and Total Control

Under Shaka's rule, the Zulu kingdom evolved into a terroristic regime, which maintained order not only through aggregative, expansionist warfare, but through the integrative mechanism of internal coercion.[19] He implemented an absolute form of centralized government, replacing hereditary chiefs of newly conquered lands with royal officials.[20] Shaka regimented everything, not just his armies. Besides military duties, he segregated men and women from one another and disallowed marriage.[21]

Shaka instituted one social reform that was a genuine innovation on his part, which dealt with female sexuality. Arranged marriages, a social establishment that survives in modern Zulu culture, determined ascendency through Shaka's centralized power structure.[22] However, as stated earlier, marriage was widely disallowed among all but the elite. Women, like men, enjoyed some sexual leniency in that they were able to take lovers so long as the actual act of intercourse did not transpire.[23] There is little hard evidence to suggest a lasting impact on Zulu birth-rates, whether legitimate or otherwise, given an already low population density[24] and the spectre of continued, aggregate warfare. However, Zulu men and women enjoyed markedly more delineated sexual relations compared to previous eras.

Sexual regulation hearkened back to the very act that despoiled Shaka's mother and resulted in his childhood ostracization. From one perspective, Shaka allowed men and women the freedom to take lovers outside of wedlock without reprisal–as long as they avoided the sins of his own parents. Some stories theorize Shaka was impotent given his animosity toward procreation,[25] as well as childhood allegations that he was physically unendowed;[26] others allege that Shaka was a serial rapist.[27] Regardless of what sexual malfunction Shaka may or may not have been afflicted by, his restrictions over sexual intercourse and procreation were probably more just another byproduct of his near-sociopathic propensity for micromanagement. The punishment for adultery (defined by actual intercourse rather than mutual masturbation and evidenced usually by unapproved pregnancies) could be as simple as cattle fines[28] and as drastic as death.[29]

Much like how modern military "boot camps" strive to break down a new recruit and refashion him or her into a proper soldier, so did Shaka's disseverment of hereditary lines and social constructs gradually wipe the slate of his subjects clean. Under stress, even the most artificial of commonalities will bring people together through relatable experiences. Over time, "the clans began to identify themselves with the Zulus, even to refer to themselves as Zulus, and the clan basis of activity began to fade."[30] This forcible unification marked the beginning of consolidated power behind the Zulu monarchy, and later guided the efforts of South African nationalist leaders in the 1960s in their pursuit of state recognition.[31]

Mfecane Uprisings

Over his eight-year rule, Dingiswayo established a Mthethwa hegemony over fifty major clans and dozens of minor ones.[32] Shaka accomplished the same over a decade, but with hundreds of clans. He became a key figure in nineteenth century European literature concerning the *mfecane* upheavals. *Mfecane*, which means "the crushing," describes a series of intense wars between 1816 and 1840, which originated in the southeastern Lowveld among the northern Nguni kingdoms of the Mthethwa, Ndwandwe, and Ngwane.[33]

Since the 1980s, however, Afrocentric historiography criticizes the *mfecane* as no more than a "propaganda myth," concocted to justify European incursion in southern Africa and drum up support from racist sympathizers back home.[34] Caricatures of African tribesmen flooded Victorian broadsheets after the massacre of British forces at Isandlwana in 1879.[35] Following the Zulu kingdom's downfall at the end of the Anglo-Zulu War, the stereotype of the partially domesticated, natural-born killer flourished in European imaginations.[36]

Certainly, the dramatic upsurge in violence occurred, but the phenomenon originated well before Shaka's era and continued long afterwards, blending easily into the patterns of violence, which accompanied increasingly militarized foreign colonization.[37] Preexisting ecological crises, including severe drought, greatly empowered Shaka's assimilation of weaker tribes into his burgeoning Zulu nation.[38] Europeans found an easy target to blame in Shaka for the *mfecane* upheavals, and his successors perpetuated his rule-through-force methodology, even though the Zulu empire quickly fragmented following Shaka's death in 1828.[39] Shaka's regimented style of military and political leadership only worked so long as he had wars to fight, and after he removed all obvious threats, "he waged war for the sake of war. . . . If he felt any goad, it was one all tyrants have discovered to their sorrow—the fact that a large standing army cannot be maintained in idleness."[40] Unfortunately for Shaka, purposeless violence begets political enemies, and his own half-brother assassinated him in 1828.[41]

Disinformation and Dehumanization

Racial bias and misinformation were not entirely one-sided. In fact, Shaka had allowed minor incursions by Europeans into Zulu territory and observed European technology, but maintained his perception of the Zulu culture's superiority throughout his reign. He even entertained European "ambassadors" (and hostages), though displayed a lack of conceptual awareness of global geography.[42] "It was perfectly obvious to all . . . that Shaka had no very clear idea who King George was or where he resided, or, in fact, what the British structure of government was . . . he thought of the white world as a large, somewhat superior, but essentially Bantu clan."[43] Shaka's half-brother (and assassin) Dingane made similar mistakes after he succeeded Shaka: attempting first to accommodate white newcomers, then rule them, and at times annihilate them, all efforts ending in varying degrees of failure.[44]

Cultural misconceptions persisted after Shaka's death, exacerbated by European antagonism. Afrikaner emigrants known as the Voortrekkers used the ongoing tension between Dingane and his rivals to establish themselves and eventually drive Dingane out.[45] They took advantage of the power vacuum left behind in the war-torn region, allocating huge tracts of land to farming and condemning thousands of South African war refugees to the south rivers.[46] The British later annexed Natal, the southern part of Zululand, in 1843. Gross mishandling of the refugee issue and territorial disputes by British colonial authorities contributed to growing anti-white sentiment among Africans.

In 1880, a Dutch trader named Cornelius Vjin published his personal memoirs of moving through the Zulu kingdom during the Anglo-Zulu wars where he periodically related friendly interactions with Zulu civilians. Yet he also noted that the Zulus feared that the British had come to export all of their males overseas for slave labor, as well as steal their cattle, and force their women into sexual slavery. "Hence," Vjin observed soberly, "when it came to fighting, [the Zulus] fought not only for [their] King only, but for themselves, since they would rather die than live under the whites."[47]

So while the Europeans stereotyped Africans as bloodthirsty savages without dignity, the Europeans were likewise stereotyped as selfish slave-traffickers who would steal their dignity. This sort of divisive dehumanization is a common tactic during periods of prolonged conflict, regardless of the historical era, but the fractious and changing sociopolitical landscape of South Africa meant these cultural biases became embedded in the region's popular history. Even now, over a century later, on average more black South Africans express disillusionment regarding interracial interactions than any other of South Africa's racial demographics—which is even more concerning given that blacks comprise close to 80 percent of South Africa's population.[48]

Us against them was a perfect unifying tactic to preserve—or, arguably, create—the African identity from European desecration. The introduction of such concepts as a cash economy and migrant work following the discoveries of diamonds and gold in southern Africa transformed economic systems and shifted population densities across the continent as surely as tribal warfare did.[49] Chiefdoms pushed back against these changes, which prompted European military responses (like the Anglo-Zulu War), and the downward spiral of economic dependency and political instability continued.[50] Another of Shaka's successors, King Cetshwayo (r. 1872 – 1879), who understood the nuanced consequences of dehumanization, complained to the same Dutch trader from before:

> Ask [the English] how I can make peace when the Queen's Army is daily capturing my cattle, burning my kraals, and killing my people? I believe that, if they go out of my country, I shall make peace with them. But, if they go on doing what they are doing, it will not be my fault if a calamity comes; and they will say, if White-men lose their lives, 'It is all Cetshwayo's doing!' whereas it is they who are doing it.[51]

Cetshwayo had the unfortunate luck to rule during a period of incredible economic change for South Africa. The discovery of gold and other precious minerals forced the region into industrialization and the capitalist market system.[52] The British viewed the Zulu kingdom, due to its economic and military independence, as an obstacle against peace and progress that they had to overcome—hence the outbreak of the Anglo-Zulu War in 1879, near the end of Cetshwayo's short reign.[53]

Heroic History and Nostalgia

Despite their bloody victory at Isandlwana, the Zulus lost the Anglo-Zulu War and their independence as a result. Racial segregationist issues which existed since the eighteenth century evolved into apartheid, "a well-articulated ideology, grounded in politics and sanctioned by religion, that asserted the superiority of one group and the inferiority of others"[54] in the twentieth century. The history of Shaka's wartime victories potentially inspired much-needed nostalgia for a simpler time when Zulu regional and cultural superiority was more easily quantified. Tales of Shaka's exploits were a fantastic source of inspiration, preserved by oral tradition, which created a "heroic history," through which the king's actions in the social system and myth become history.[55] Praise poetry for King Shaka continues to be popular, and maintains relevance as commentary upon the growing complexities of black/white political engagements and the processes of modernization.[56]

King Shaka International Airport opened in May 2010 and became the brief focus of controversy following the short-lived placement of a statue depicting King Shaka as a herd-boy in front of the airport.[57] KwaZulu-Natal celebrates Shaka Day every year. All efforts to demonize Shaka and his military gains by nineteenth century European media served the opposite effect in South Africa. The modern Zulu people have since appropriated and romanticized the same aspects of Shaka's personality which once inspired trepidation, derision, and a sense of racist superiority among colonists and their contemporaries in Europe. The mythos surrounding Shaka and the Zulu identity shaped African politics, specifically the approaches of political groups such as the African National Congress and the Pan Africanist Congress, and armed struggle against apartheid.

Recently, the Zulu identity, and Shaka's role within it, appears as nebulous as it does enduring. Dr. S. Nombuso Dlamini, Research Leadership Chair at the University of Windsor, based much of her conclusions on youth and identity politics in South Africa on her observations of willing participants in the youth community. She observed, for instance, that students associated the use of the Zulu language with illiteracy or ignorance, especially in academic settings where speaking English was encouraged.[58] This dichotomy would be indicative of a greater identity conflict, in which being more (or less) Zulu becomes a point of contest, drawing the group together, but also creating an artificial isolation. Using individual cases to illustrate, Dlamini noted the impact of the Shaka mythos on the rationalization of personal identity and history:

> For Vukani, who is still actively involved in the MK [*Umkhonto we Sizwe*, an armed wing of the African National Congress], it became important for him not to denounce the Shakan wars of conquest because it was through the wars that his military practices could be legitimized. To Ndabezitha and Lunga, the myth of Shaka and the consolidation of the Zulu kingdom were important because, as descendants of those who fought these consolidation wars, they were positioned as more Zulu than others (*Zulu Zu*), which implied they were direct products of these acts of bravery.[59]

Shaka's military exploits and sociopolitical reconstruction of the Zulu Kingdom during a critical, foundational point in South African history were crucial elements in creating the Zulu identity. However, without excusing the practices, the persistence of the Zulu identity must also pay credit to the dehumanizing components of European colonialism, racial segregation, and apartheid. Dehumanization not only engendered an *us versus them* environment which forced people together under a tenuously shared banner of tribal identity, but inadvertently romanticized the stories of King Shaka and ensured his character a permanent fixture in South African popular history.

Notes

1. "A Warm Welcome to KwaZulu-Natal – Tourism KwaZulu-Natal," Tourism KwaZulu-Natal, 2014, accessed July 11, 2015, http://www.zulu.org.za/about/key-facts/welcome.

2. Ibid.

3. Ana Maria Monteiro-Ferreira, "Reevaluating Zulu Religion: An Afrocentric Analysis," *Journal of Black Studies* 35, No. 3 (January 2005): 348, accessed June 28, 2015, http://www.jstor.org/stable/40034764.

4. James L. Gibson, "Apartheid's Long Shadow: How Racial Divides Distort South Africa's Democracy," *Foreign Affairs* 94, No. 2 (March/April 2015): 42.

5. Mathieu Deflem, "Warfare, political leadership, and state formation: The case of the Zulu Kingdom, 1808-1879," *Ethnology* 38, no. 4 (Fall 1999): 5, accessed June 28, 2015, http://search.proquest.com/docview/205102576?accountid=8289.

6. E. A. Ritter, *Shaka Zulu* (Harmondsworth: Penguin Books, 1987), 26.

7. Donald R. Morris, *The Washing of the Spears: A History of the Rise of the Zulu Nation under Shaka and Its Fall in the Zulu War of 1879* (New York: Simon & Schuster, Inc., 1965), 44.

8. Deflem, 5.

9. Dan Wylie, *Myth of Iron: Shaka in History* (Athens: Ohio University Press, 2006), 19.

10. Sibusisiwe Nombuso Dlamini, *Youth and Identity Politics in South Africa, 1990-1994* (Toronto: University of Toronto Press, 2005), 7, accessed October 24, 2015, available through Google Books.

11. Ibid.

12. Morris, 51; Deflem, 7.

13. Benedict Carton and Robert Morell, "Zulu Masculinities, Warrior Culture and Stick Fighting," *Journal of Southern African Studies* 38, No. 1 (March 2012): 33, accessed June 28, 2015, available through APUS library resources.

14. Morris, 47.

15. Wylie, 125.

16. Ibid, 186-187.

17. Deflem, 5.

18. Morris, 47.

19. Deflem, 8.

20. Kevin Shillington, *History of Africa* (New York: St Martin's Press, 2012), 265.

21. Ibid, 266; Morris, 66.

22. Wylie, 329.

23. Ibid, 328-329.

24. Deflem, 8.

25. Morris, 91.

26. Ibid, 45.

27. Wylie, 138-139.

28. Morris, 66.

29. Wylie, 322.

30. Morris, 64.

31. Dlamini, 7-8.

32. Ibid, 42.

33. Shillington, 263.

34. Ibid; Carton et al, 36.

35. Carton et al, 34-35.

36. Ibid.

37. Wylie, 439.

38. Dlamini, 32.

39. Monteiro-Ferreira, 351; Deflem, 10.

40. Morris, 64-65.

41. Shillington, 267.

42. Morris, 97; Wylie, 321.

43. Morris, 97.

44. Dlamini, 33.

45. Ibid.

46. Ibid.

47. Cornelius Vijn, *Cetshwayo's Dutchman,* trans. John W. Colenso (London: Longmans, Green, and Co, 1880), 15, accessed July 11, 2015, https://archive.org/details/cetshwayosdutchm00cornrich.

48. Gibson, 42-46.

49. Shillington, 329.

50. Ibid, 332.

51. Vijn, 47.

52. Dlamini, 34.

53. Ibid.

54. Gibson, 44.

55. Deflem, 9.

56. Michael Chapman, "From Shaka's Court to the Trade Union Rally: Praises in a Usable Past," *Research in African Literatures* 30, No. 1 (Spring 1999): 4-6, accessed June 28, 2015, http://search.proquest.com/docview/207644878?accountid=8289.

57. "Thank Shaka for Zulu Identity," *Independent Online*, September 25, 2010, accessed July 12, 2015, http://www.iol.co.za/news/politics/thank-shaka-for-zulu-identity-1.681694#.VaLMWPlViko.

58. Dlamini, 128.

59. Ibid, 191.

Bibliography

"A Warm Welcome to KwaZulu-Natal – Tourism KwaZulu-Natal." *Tourism KwaZulu-Natal.* 2014. Accessed July 11, 2015. http://www.zulu.org.za/about/key-facts/welcome.

Carton, Benedict and Robert Morell. "Zulu Masculinities, Warrior Culture and Stick Fighting." *Journal of Southern African Studies* 38, No. 1 (March 2012). Accessed June 28, 2015. Available through APUS library resources.

Chapman, Michael. "From Shaka's Court to the Trade Union Rally: Praises in a Usable Past." *Research in African Literatures* 30, No. 1 (Spring 1999). Accessed June 28, 2015. http://search.proquest.com/docview/207644878?accountid=8289.

Deflem, Mathieu. "Warfare, political leadership, and state formation: The case of the Zulu Kingdom, 1808-1879." *Ethnology* 38, no. 4 (Fall 1999). Accessed June 28, 2015. http://search.proquest.com/docview/205102576?accountid=8289.

Gibson, James L. "Apartheid's Long Shadow: How Racial Divides Distort South Africa's Democracy." *Foreign Affairs* 94, No. 2 (March/April 2015): 42-46.

Monteiro-Ferreira, Ana Maria. "Reevaluating Zulu Religion: An Afrocentric Analysis." *Journal of Black Studies* 35, No. 3 (January 2005). Accessed June 28, 2015. http://www.jstor.org/stable/40034764/.

Morris, Donald R. *The Washing of the Spears: A History of the Rise of the Zulu Nation under Shaka and Its Fall in the Zulu War of 1879.* New York: Simon & Schuster, Inc., 1965.

Nombuso Dlamini, Sibusisiwe. *Youth and Identity Politics in South Africa, 1990-1994.* Toronto: University of Toronto Press, 2005. Accessed October 24, 2015. Available through Google Books.

Ritter, E. A. *Shaka Zulu.* Harmondsworth: Penguin Books, 1987.

"Thank Shaka for Zulu Identity." *Independent Online.* September 25, 2010. Accessed July 12, 2015. http://www.iol.co.za/news/politics/thank-shaka-for-zulu-identity-1.681694#.VaLMWPlViko.

Vijn, Cornelius. *Cetshwayo's Dutchman.* Translated by John W. Colenso. London: Longmans, Green, and Co, 1880. Accessed June 28, 2015. https://archive.org/details/cetshwayosdutchm00cornrich.

Wylie, Dan. *Myth of Iron: Shaka in History.* Athens: Ohio University Press, 2006.

Huguenots and the French Enlightenment

Allison Ramsey

The seventeenth and eighteenth century European Enlightenment movement sparked a fundamental reorientation in attitudes toward human reason and political, social, and individual rights. However, it was also a time of religious upheaval in France. The Catholic and Protestant religious groups, working along with the wishes of the monarchy, struggled to find a way to coexist. When Louis XIV inherited the throne in 1643, the French Protestants, or Huguenots, found themselves in a difficult situation. The Sun King effectively ended all hope for Protestantism in France with the Edict of Fontainebleau—or the Revocation of the Edict of Nantes—in 1685. Even though Catholics and Protestants alike were weary of fighting within the country, they could not agree upon a peaceable co-existence. This led to a grand migration of Protestants in search of a better life in other areas of the world. Eventually, with the help of popular philosophe opinion, the Huguenots regained many of their individual rights in France, even though these were reluctantly given. While the Enlightenment represented a growth in personal freedom for many, it was a time of fluctuation, instability, and turmoil for the Huguenots.

A study of the troubles of the French Protestants could logically start with the Revocation of the Edict of Nantes. Henry IV issued the original policy in April of 1598 in an attempt to bring peace during the turmoil of the French Wars of Religion (1562-1598) and it included civil rights and an amount of tolerance toward the Protestant religion heretofore unknown. It permitted "those of the said religion called Reformed to live and abide in all the cities and places of this our kingdom and countries of our sway, without being annoyed, molested, or compelled to do anything in the matter of religion contrary to their consciences."[1] Unfortunately, neither the Catholics nor the Protestants were entirely satisfied with the contents of the edict. This would change when Louis XIV (r. 1643-1715) took the throne.

The Huguenots found themselves in a difficult situation following Louis XIV's accession. Upon the urging of the Catholic Church, the new king slowly and methodically introduced new measures that rescinded French Calvinist rights. It was hoped that by reducing their freedoms, the Huguenots would be persuaded to simply convert through self-interest.[2] The ex-Huguenot Paul Pellisson was charged with leading a *Caisse des Conversions*, which was meant to reward Protestants willing to convert to Catholicism. This financial program offered social and educational support to converts, and provided funding that converts could use to build new homes.[3] Additionally, Versailles encouraged dialogue between the embittered rival theologians in an effort to bridge the gap between their opposing creeds. Finally, and most dramatically, Intendant Nicolas-Joseph Foucault of Bearn initiated the *grande dragonnade*. This group swept through southern France in 1681 and in May of 1685, battling in the major strongholds of Huguenot power.[4] In the past, dragoons had aided in forcible conversions, but this was secondary to other acts, such as responding to armed rebellions. The *grande dragonnade*, however, had the sole purpose of forcing Protestants in even the most remote places in France to convert. Soldiers lodging with Protestants until they finally abjured achieved this goal.[5]

The Edict of Fontainebleau, presented on October 22, 1685, ended all rights for the Huguenots and their religion, referred to as the *Religion Prétendue Réformée*, or "alleged religion," within the edict. It stated,

> And since by this fact the execution of the Edict of Nantes and of all that has ever been ordained in favor of the said R.P.R. has been rendered nugatory, we have determined that we can do nothing better, in order wholly to obliterate the memory of the troubles, the confusion, and the evils which the progress of this false religion has caused in this kingdom, and which furnished occasion for the said edict and for so many previous and subsequent edicts and declarations, than entirely to revoke the Edict of Nantes, with the special articles granted as a sequel to it, as well as all that has since been done in favor of the said religion.[6]

The severe penalties exacted with the Revocation of the Edict of Nantes led to a lifestyle that was uncertain at best for the Protestant people living in France. Studying the relationship between Catholics and Huguenots during the Enlightenment requires navigation through frequently murky waters. Even though there were obvious religious and political differences between the French Catholics and Protestants, the reality of the situation often showed them working together in a neighborly setting. Dr. Keith P. Luria, history professor at North Carolina State University and published author, suggested, "familial, social, business, intellectual, and political contacts produced shared concerns."[7] In such a turbulent time period in history both groups would have been eager to keep peace between themselves. The French people as a whole were crippled and worn out from their wartime exertions. Another element to consider was the strength each group had within their communities. If the Catholics were the dominant group, the Protestants would more than likely have changed their mannerisms enough to peaceably coexist within their neighborhood. The reverse could also have been true. In areas where Protestantism was prevalent, the Catholic community would have had a harder time reestablishing their ways of worship.[8] In addition, outsiders were able to impact relations between the two religious groups. For example, royal officials would have been on hand to ensure both remembered the importance of following the king's wishes for peace within his realm.[9]

For every situation where outsiders acted as peacekeepers between the two groups, there was an adverse situation where they acted as interlopers. Missionaries sought to light a fire under their religious counterparts, stirring up controversy and provoking conflict. The groups were often unable to come to peaceable terms concerning the sharing of local power, the partition of communal sacred space, or their respective religious observances.[10] Catherine Randall, senior lecturer for the Department of Religion at Dartmouth, summed up the situation succinctly when she stated, "Even if the Revocation of the Edict of Nantes put the Protestants in peril, it was not able to eliminate them or their beliefs. Louis XIV, intending to wipe out with one stroke of his pen this irritating religious anomaly in his kingdom, succeeded only in creating serious internal and external political problems."[11]

The Huguenots were persecuted in many different areas of daily life. The Edict of Nantes did little to curb the hatred the Catholics held for the Protestants. For example, a man naming a Protestant place of worship as a "church" could be fined up to 500 livres. In Rouen, a Protestant youth was not able to be apprenticed until fourteen Roman Catholics were taken in. They were forbidden to sing psalms, forced to bury their dead in the middle of the night, and unable to send their children to anything more than minor schools in which they were merely taught to read, write, and count.[12] Protestant churches were pulled down in alarming numbers, forcing church members to travel great distances, at times forty or more miles, in order to attend services or to have their children baptized.[13]

These are just a few examples included on a lengthy list of reasons why the Huguenots were receptive to the idea of leaving France in large numbers. According to Charles Nicholas de la Cherois Purdon's 1865 series regarding French settlers in Ireland, three thousand families left during a single quarter in 1682.[14] The Revocation affected 730,000 French Protestants.[15] An estimated 150,000 to 180,000 individuals escaped the country between 1680 and 1700.[16] The emigration of the Huguenots spanned a large portion of the globe. They settled in many locations outside of France during the Enlightenment including North and South Carolina,

Virginia, New York, and Massachusetts in North America. The Huguenot settlements in North America reaped both positive and negative consequences.

Many Huguenots looked to the lands across the Atlantic as a place where they could escape persecution and find reprieve from political and religious turmoil.[17] However, their adversities and misfortunes did not end with relocation to new areas. A new Languedoc arrival to Boston wrote back to his friends in France, "You must disabuse yourself of the Impression that Advantages are here offered to Refugees . . . Whoever brings Nothing, finds Nothing."[18] Huguenots in the New England area found themselves in the middle of a battleground of spiritual and literal warfare, with French Protestants and French Catholics both fighting for dominance over Native American missionary conversions.[19] This was in addition to fighting off the English in an effort to gain Native American resources and converts.

Despite these initial hardships in moving to North America, the Huguenots were able to thrive in their new environment, and as the Huguenot refugee Charles de Sailly wrote in July of 1700 to an English colleague, "We are, thank God, in a fine and beautiful country, where, after the first difficulties, we shall live well and happily."[20] As time went on, the colonies, and Pennsylvania in particular, attracted the attention of the French philosophes for the religious freedom for which they had fought. Then, in 1776, the United States offered a revolutionary approach to dealing with the centuries-old dilemma of state religions. The newly formed country decided that individuals could choose on their own what they would believe and practice with a separation of church and state. Marquis de Lafayette, an instrumental general in the Revolutionary War, acted as a link between the new religious freedom in the United States and the fight for Huguenot relief in France. According to Concordia University's former History Chair, Geoffrey Adams, "his admiration for Washington played no small part in his decision to join the lobby working to achieve in France the kind of religious freedom the Americans had fought to confirm."[21]

While the Protestant refugees received a mixed welcome from the colonists in North America, several European countries had provided a warmer welcome over the years. In the late sixteenth century, entire regiments of Huguenots were sent by William, Prince of Orange, to accompany him to England and Ireland. After the peace was restored in these areas, many of the Protestant soldiers stayed and several new settlements were formed.[22] An example of this can be found at Youghal, Ireland, where the parish registers record the prefixes "Cornet," "Ensign," "Levt.," and "Captain."[23] Shortly after the Edict of Nantes was signed, large numbers moved into Switzerland, Germany, England, and

Holland. The Queen of Denmark and the Swiss showed the greatest sympathy and received all who came. In Holland, those who had served in the French army were offered commissions equal to their prior rank in their new country of residence.

Despite their past issues, the Huguenots prospered in many areas. Linsburn in the county of Antrim, Ireland, was one particularly successful Huguenot community. The Irish King invited Louis Crommelin and his son, refugees living in Holland, to settle the area as a linen manufacturing center. They brought with them a number of Huguenot refugees and began a colony. A church was built and the services conducted in French for the benefit of the community.[24]

Meanwhile, back in France, the Enlightenment movement flourished and, with it, came support for the Huguenots in the form of the philosophes who were gaining in popularity throughout the country. They were ambassadors for toleration and individual rights, which easily translated into the reintegration of the Huguenots into the national community.[25] Huguenot assimilation into other countries did not go unnoticed by the popular thinkers and writers of the Enlightenment. Baron Charles Montesquieu, who believed more in morality than in religious devotion, and Voltaire, who believed in tolerance, were particularly vociferous about the situation and religious pluralism in the "Protestant North." For example, during the summer of 1765, Voltaire wrote of growing support in a letter to Claude-Adrien Helvétius, aspiring poet and disciple of the philosopher, "All the North is with us . . . Russia, Poland, Austria and Prussia have raised the banners of toleration and philosophy. . . . We French are obviously not destined to be first in these matters; truths reach us from abroad; but even if such truths come to us from outside, it is, of course, excellent that we should adopt them."[26]

By the early 1760s, French policy regarding the Protestants began to change. Physical repression stopped almost entirely and the King's ministers started seeing reason in the philosophes' desire to promote a spiritually open society.[27] Spain was the last symbol of the "medieval" past where, Adams remarked, "state and church conspired to crush the spirit."[28] Voltaire, along with other philosophes of the time, would have been dismayed to see their country keeping company with another that most considered so backward. Antoine Court's 1760 publication, *Histoire des Troubles des Cévennes,* mentioned the failure of forced religious conversions, stating, "instead of making Catholics, [it] made libertines, faithless men, atheists and finally rebels."[29]

The French Protestants finally felt some relief when the Edict of Toleration was introduced in November of 1787. The wording showcased the reluctance of the government to change its ways and stubbornly admitted that the Huguenots deserved to enjoy at least some rights as French subjects. This is most easily seen in paragraph four, which stated,

> The Catholic religion that we have the good fortune to profess will alone enjoy in our kingdom the rights and honors of public worship, while our other, non-Catholic subjects, deprived of all influence on the established order in our state, declared in advance and forever ineligible for forming a separate body within our kingdom, and subject to the ordinary police [and not their own clergy] for the observation of religious festival days, will only get from the law what natural right does not permit us to refuse them, to register their births, their marriages and their deaths, in order to enjoy, like all our other subjects, the civil effects that result from this.[30]

Even so, the Edict of Toleration gave the Protestants, along with other religious groups, the same rights the Catholics had enjoyed all along. Following in the footsteps of the Americans and their separation of church and state, the French finally showed the same tolerance and allowed the Huguenots to practice their religion in peace. The edict allowed current and future residents of the state to enjoy all goods and rights regardless of their religious beliefs. It also gave people of all religions the right to pursue commerce, arts, crafts, and professions without discrimination.[31]

The philosophes gave strength and voice to oppressed commoners in France during the Enlightenment, although it took quite some time for the movement to aid in the plight of the Huguenots. The persecution of these families fueled a massive emigration from France into much of Europe and eastern North America. The acts of countries like the United States and Ireland, and individuals like Lafayette and Voltaire, did a great deal to further the cause of the French Protestants. The Huguenots and their ordeal represent the fluctuating nature of religious tolerance that was a defining characteristic of the Enlightenment movement of the eighteenth century.

Notes

1. James Harvey Robinson, ed., *Readings in European History* 2 vols. (Boston: Ginn, 1906), 2:183-185, accessed December 29, 2013, http://www.historyguide.org/earlymod/nantes.html.

2. Geoffrey Adams, *Huguenots and French Opinion 1685-1787: The Enlightenment Debate on Toleration* (Waterloo: Wilfrid Laurier University Press, 1991), 197, accessed December 21, 2013, http://site.ebrary.com/lib/apus/docDetail.action?docID=10147235.

3. Marianne Carbonnier-Burkard and Patrick Cabanal, *Une Histoire des Protestants en France* (Paris : Desclée de Brouwer, 1998), accessed August 15, 2015, http://www.museeprotestant.org/notice/la-politique-de-conversion-1660-1685/.

4. Adams, *Huguenots and the French Opinion,* 197.

5. Christie Sample Wilson, *Beyond Belief: Surviving the Revocation of the Edict of Nantes in France* (Lanham: Lehigh University Press, 2011), 64.

6. Isambert, *Recueil général des anciennes lois françaises* XIX, 530 *sqq*, translated in J.H. Robinson, *Readings in European History* 2 vols. (Boston: Ginn, 1906), 2:180-183, accessed December 28, 2013, Web.

7. Keith P. Luria, *Sacred Boundaries: Religious Coexistence and Conflict in Early Modern France* (Washington DC: Catholic University of America Press, 2005), 1, accessed December 22, 2013, http://site.ebrary.com/lib/apus/docDetail.action?docID=10267233.

8. Ibid., 2.

9. Ibid., 3.

10. Ibid., 2.

11. Catharine Randall, *From a Far Country: Camisards and Huguenots in the Atlantic World* (Athens: University of Georgia Press, 2009), 11, accessed December 26, 2013, http://site.ebrary.com/lib/apus/docDetail.action?docID=10367027.

12. Charles Nicholas de la Cherois Purdon, "The French Settlers in Ireland, No. 1. The Huguenot Colony at Lisburn, County of Antrim," *Ulster Journal of Archaeology,* first series, volume 1, (1853): 209-210, accessed December 5, 2013, http://www.jstor.org/stable/20563463.

13. Ibid., 210.

14. de la Cherois Purdon, "The French Settlers in Ireland," 210.

15. David E. Lambert, *Studies in Church History, Volume 12: Protestant International and the Huguenot Migration to Virginia,* (New York: Peter Lang, 2009), 26, accessed December 29, 2013, http://site.ebrary.com/lib/apus/docDetail.action?docID=10516914.

16. Ibid., 27.

17. Owen Stanwood, "Between Eden and Empire: Huguenot Refugees and the Promise of New Worlds," *American Historical Review,* volume 118, issue 5, (2013): 1326, accessed July 1, 2015, http://search.ebscohost.com/login.aspx?direct=true&db=tsh&AN=92875086&site=ehost-live&scope=site.

18. Randall, *From a Far Country,* 61.

19. Stanwood, "Between Eden and Empire," 1336.

20. Lambert, *Studies in Church History,* 2.

21. Adams, *Huguenots and the French Opinion,* 197-198.

22. de la Cherois Purdon, "The French Settlers in Ireland," 211.

23. Samuel Hayman, "The French Settlers in Ireland, No. 4. The Settlement at Youghal, County Cork," *Ulster Journal of Archaeology,* first series, volume 2, (1854), 224, accessed December

5, 2013, http://www.jstor.org/stable/20608731.

24. de la Cherois Purdon, "The French Settlers in Ireland," 212.

25. Adams, *Huguenots and the French Opinion,* 197.

26. Ibid.

27. Ibid., 201.

28. Ibid., 197.

29. Antoine Court, *Histoire des troubles des Cévennes, ou de la guerre des Camisars, sous le régne de Louis le Grand; tirée de manuscrits secrets et autentiques et des obvervations faites sur les lieux memes, avec une carte des Cévennes,* volume 3, (Villefranche: P. Chrétrien, 1760), quoted in Adams, *Huguenots and the French Opinion,* 200.

30. *The French Revolution and Human Rights: A Brief Documentary History,* translated, edited, and with an introduction by Lynn Hunt (Boston/New York: Bedford/St. Martin's, 1996), 40-43, accessed December 28, 2013, Web.

31. Ibid.

Bibliography

Adams, Geoffrey. *Huguenots and French Opinion 1685-1787: The Enlightenment Debate on Toleration*. Waterloo: Wilfrid Laurier University Press, 1991. Accessed December 5, 2013. http://site.ebrary.com/lib/apus/ docDetail.action?docID=10147235.

Carbonnier-Burkard, Marianne, and Patrick Cabanal. *Une Histoire des Protestants en France*. Paris: Desclée de Brouwer, 1998. Accessed August 15, 2015. http://www.museeprotestant.org/notice/la-politique-de-conversion-1660-1685/.

de la Cherois Purdon, Charles Nicholas. "The French Settlers in Ireland. No. 1. The Huguenot Colony at Lisburn, County of Antrim." *Ulster Journal of Archaeology*. First Series, Volume 1 (1853). Accessed December 5, 2013. http://www.jstor.org/stable/20563463.

Hayman, Samuel. "The French Settlers in Ireland. No. 4. The Settlement at Youghal, County Cork." *Ulster Journal of Archaeology*. First Series, Volume 2 (1854). Accessed December 5, 2013. http://www.jstor.org/ stable/20608731.

Hunt, Lynn, trans. *The French Revolution and Human Rights: A Brief Documentary History*. Boston: Bedford/ St. Martin's, 1996. Accessed December 28, 2013. Web.

Isambert. *Recueil général des anciennes lois françaises* XIX, 530 *sqq*. Translated in J.H. Robinson. *Readings in European History* 2 vols. Boston: Ginn, 1906. Accessed December 28, 2013. Web.

Lambert, David E. *Studies in Church History, Volume 12: Protestant International and the Huguenot Migration to Virginia*. New York: Peter Lang, 2009. Accessed December 29, 2013. http://site.ebrary.com/lib/apus/ docDetail.action?docID=10516914.

Luria, Keith P. *Sacred Boundaries: Religious Coexistence and Conflict in Early-Modern France*. Washington, DC: Catholic University of America Press, 2005. Accessed December 5, 2013. http://site.ebrary.com/lib/apus/ docDetail.action?docID=10267233.

Randall, Catharine. *From a Far Country: Camisards and Huguenots in the Atlantic World*. Athens: University of Georgia Press, 2009. Accessed December 26, 2013. http://site.ebrary.com/lib/apus/docDetail.action? docID=10367027.

Robinson, James Harvey, ed. *Readings in European History* 2 vols. Boston: Ginn, 1906. Accessed December 29, 2013. http://www.historyguide.org/

earlymod/nantes.html.

Stanwood, Owen. "Between Eden and Empire: Huguenot Refugees and the Promise of New Worlds." *American Historical Review,* Volume 118, Issue 5 (2013). Accessed July 1, 2015. http://search.ebscohost.com/ login.aspx?direct=true&db=tsh&AN=92875086&site=ehost-live&scope=site.

Wilson, Christie Sample. *Beyond Belief: Surviving the Revocation of the Edict of Nantes in France.* Lanham: Lehigh University Press, 2011.

A Democratic Consideration of Herodotus's *Histories*

Mary Jo Davies

In the *Histories*, Herodotus's admiration of Athenian Democracy is apparent when he compares a strong, democratic Athens in the fifth century BC to monarchies and tyrannies. Compelled to satisfy the needs or decisions of kings and tyrants, Persian soldiers became compulsory participants, which often transmuted into disasters on the battlefield. On the contrary, Athenian democracy's anti-aristocratic arrangement promoted cooperative decision-making for the interest of the community. This freedom encouraged soldiers to become willing participants in warfare. Although victory was not always in their hands, to Herodotus, fighting for the collective interest of a community rather than for the narcissistic pursuit of one leader fostered an unwavering commitment to the cause. Inspired by Athenian ways of expressing egalitarian values, Herodotus's intention for writing the *Histories* was not to give Greece a sense of its historical identity, but to endorse the advantages of democratic rule over tyranny. This paper will prove that Herodotus's purpose for writing the *Histories* was to promote democracy.

Historiography and Sources

In her article, "Athenian Democratic Ideology and Herodotus' *Histories*" Sara Forsdyke proposed a new evaluation of Herodotus's *Histories* by establishing a thematic connection between tyranny and civic weakness versus democratic freedom and civic strength. Drawing on a substantial amount of primary source literature, Forsdyke concluded that each character and event represents a reflection of democratic principles. This offers a valuable starting point to analyze further Herodotus's *Histories* as propaganda for endorsing democracy.

Herodotus is recognized as the first Western historian. There is no prior written evidence to contradict him or his methodology. Hence, his propensity for exaggerating and even creating some of the events he chronicled.[1] As a consequence, reliability for historical military accuracy becomes sketchy at best. Historians Everett Wheeler and Barry Strauss also recognized Herodotus's limitations when they state that Herodotus "puts [words] in Mardonius's mouth."[2] In "Can We Trust the Ancient Texts," Richard A. Gabriel analyzes the propensity for ancient Greek and Roman historians, such as Herodotus and Livy, to fabricate evidence. They were less concerned with conveying truthful accounts than they were with teaching moral lessons.[3] In light of this, it is plausible to surmise that

Herodotus's underlying intention for writing the *Histories* was to endorse the advantages of democratic rule over tyranny.

Democracy in ancient Athens cannot be compared to modern standards of social equity. It was not as inclusive as contemporary democracies. Most people in ancient Athens, including women, slaves, foreigners, and the very poor, had few civil rights and civil liberties. The adult male citizens of modest to wealthy standing were the only class that retained extraordinary control over the city's political affairs. Despite this social inequity, it was from this perspective that Herodotus trusted democracy's ability to foster communal strength and intelligence. He believed it to be the most powerful medium for uniting all of Greece against future threats. Indeed, Herodotus was the first person to use the unifying term *Hellas* to define all people living in the Greek-speaking world. Motivated by Athenian ways of expressing political ideals, it is easy to suppose that Herodotus breathed new life into the various historical personages to befit his admiration of democracy.

Background

Herodotus was born in Halicarnassus, a Greek city located on the western coast of modern-day Turkey. Based on bits of evidence scattered throughout his writings, it is possible to determine that he was born around the year 485 BC. The Greco-Persian wars he wrote about took place within a fifty-year period beginning fourteen years prior to his determined birth. Consequently, it is necessary to assume that stories of the earlier years of the war were based on accounts that were handed down to him by his elders. Herodotus also did not participate in any war. That he lacked the advantage of eyewitness evidence further justifies the case for embellishment.

A Democratic Agenda

Whether or not the speeches or conversations recorded in the *Histories* are historically accurate is, as discussed above, questionable. However, since Herodotus was using those stories to promote democracy, they may very well represent a juxtaposition between freedom and tyranny. For example, in his quest to punish the Athenians for past aggressions, Persian king Xerxes demanded complete commitment from his troops. To that end he ordered, "When I tell you that it's time to come, you must all rush to come."[4] However, retrospective, word-for-word dialogues are not possible to recount, especially when, like Herodotus, one is not present at the event. Lacking the verification to prove that Xerxes actually said this, one can easily make the leap and presume that Herodotus's intent was to highlight Persian civic weakness.[5]

Herodotus did not limit his fabrications to conversations and speeches. To further promote democracy, he also exaggerated the number of enemy soldiers and military fatalities. When Persian military commander Mardonius says that he does not believe the Greeks "will learn how far beyond other men we are in the skills of war,"[6] Herodotus is setting the reader up for an ironic twist of military success. The Greek army, significantly smaller, defeated the Persians at the battle of Salamis in 480 BC. Although all Greeks at Salamis fought as one Panhellenic army, victory according to Herodotus belonged to the Athenians. The Athenians were the ones who rallied all the Greeks in the Hellenic world to fight against the Persians. Hence, what seems like straightforward chronicling of military history can easily become a reflection of a political and cultural approach to understanding warfare. According to Herodotus, Athenian democracy promoted the willingness to fight for the preservation of freedom, where men fought for their own interests rather than the interest of a single ruler.[7] On the contrary, the Persian soldiers fought under penalty of execution. Indeed, the very word "freedom," its equivalents and any concept associated with liberty did not exist in ancient Persia. Democracy's freedom and the unifying strength fostered by it could have been the very things that Herodotus hoped would inspire non-democratic Greek societies to convert and become one cohesive empire. For the time being however, while all Greeks at Salamis fought for the preservation of their freedom from Persian control, Athenians (and any other city-state ruled by democracy) lived that political freedom off the battlefield, in their daily lives.

Sparta was still a monarchy. Although they had evolved into an outstanding warrior race, they stubbornly resisted the cultural innovations that characterized Athens. With a small population and a stagnant economy, their primary aim was to bolster their size, stabilize their wealth, and create an efficient army through rigorous military training. To that end, they made allies of many of their neighbors. Subsequently, they enslaved the Messenians to work in the fields and confiscated their wealth to bolster their economy.[8] But to Herodotus, Sparta lacked the cooperative intelligence as fostered by a democracy. Though Sparta's participation at the battle of Salamis provided the necessary courage for Greek triumph, without Athens's rallying spirit of democracy, Herodotus believed that Sparta's allies would have left them to stand alone against their enemy.[9] Thus it does not matter how much larger the Persian army was than the Greek army (the numbers are surely exaggerated), or if the Salamis account is even historically accurate. The battle of Salamis, as told by Herodotus, reveals the value of a democratic culture, which he believed was the only way to unite all of Greece against the enemy.

At times, it was enough for Herodotus to describe the cause for the limitations of a monarchy to prove his point. The interview between Lydian King Croesus and Solon of Athens provides an ideal example. Though Solon was a tyrant who ruled in 560 BC prior to the establishment of democracy, his reign included the founding of new laws, which would eventually serve as a model for Athenian democracy.[10] Thus, the philosophical conversation between Solon and Croesus highlighted the Athenian leader's intellectual disposition versus the pompous nature of the Lydian king who considered his own happiness and good fortune worthy of honor. Presented as the wise Athenian, Solon understood how fickle fortune was and refused to honor the Lydian king with the title of "happy." According to Solon, only men who retain all the blessings of life until the end of their lives deserved to be honored with that title.[11]

Equally revealing is the story of imperial corruption. To demonstrate his point, Herodotus highlighted the depravity of Spartan kings Cleomenes and Leotychides. Sparta traditionally had two kings. Cleomenes's hostility toward his co-regent, Demaratus, would eventually play a major role in his own demise. Yet, tension also existed between Demaratus and his cousin Leotychides, who aspired to the throne. Reviving an old rumor that Demaratus was the illegitimate son of King Ariston, Cleomenes and Leotychides both conspired and succeeded in forcing Demaratus out. Thus, in the fifth century BC, Leotychides became co-regent of Sparta alongside Cleomenes. Although Demaratus's mother told her son that he was in actual fact the legitimate son of his father and rightful heir to the throne, he was compelled to flee the country. Historically branded a turncoat, he joined Xerxes to fight against his own people. Eventually Leotychides was exposed for bribery and banished from his kingdom. He escaped to Tegea where he eventually died.[12] Cleomenes, who in his conspiracy had forced the Delphic oracle to lie in favor of Leotychides, was now in fear for his own life. He fled Sparta with the Lacedaemonians on his tail and later died a gruesome death by self-mutilation to avoid punishment. It is no accident that Herodotus praised Athenian democracy immediately before this vivid account of imperial treachery.[13]

Whether or not these stories are factual is irrelevant; the underlying motive for including them in his accounts reveals what Herodotus believed could never happen in a democratic society. In the process, he gave his audience a glimpse of everything that was negative of life under a monarchy, where pompous kings believed they were worthy of veneration and where corrupt kings took the throne by way of deceit and died in disgrace. Moreover, unaccustomed to exercising their intellect, or simply uninformed, the people living under a monarch more readily blamed the death of their ruler on punishment from the gods or excessive drink. They were not freely disposed to consider the failings of monarchies and tyrannies or the advantages of democracies. It is clear that Herodotus was aware of the struggle that was building between democratic Athens and oligarchic Sparta. This tension would eventually lead to the Peloponnesian war in 431 BC and turn the tides in Spartan favor with devastating consequences for Athens. Perhaps in foreseeing this, Herodotus hoped, through his writings, to prevent it.[14]

Herodotus on Women

Although women in Athens were not participatory citizens, they were, nevertheless, a complimentary part of the whole. Athenian democracy was fashioned not just by men, but by women through men. Women needed to be respectable representatives of Athenian democracy in accordance with their status, but to better understand Herodotus's treatment of women in the *Histories*, it is necessary to become acquainted with the condition of women in classical Athenian society.

An Athenian woman's intelligence was not based on her own inherent acumen. Fifth century historian Xenophon discusses proper Athenian female etiquette at length in the *Economics*. In it, the principle character Ischomachus speaks with admiration of his wife's intelligence, but he is not referring to her level of competence nor is he commenting on her breadth of worldly knowledge. He is revealing her astute ability to obey and learn and by consequence, he is boasting of his own ability to teach.[15]

This type of patriarchal reality was pervasive even in comedy. Fifth century BC comic playwright Aristophanes repeatedly placed his female characters where Athenian democratic society forbade them to be — outdoors. Acting in a manner that countered acceptable behavior, they undertook and accomplished things they would never have been able to accomplish in real life. In *Ecclesiazusae*, women disguised themselves as men to attend the assembly and demand that women should run the country. It might be tempting to believe that Aristophanes was giving women in the real world the incentive to rise up to the occasion. After all, women did win the right to rule the country in his play. However, in antiquity men performed the role of women on stage. Indeed, in *Ecclesiazusae*, men played women dressed as men. Equally revealing is the fact that Aristophanes allowed women to win the right to rule the country by men who, in turn, agreed to surrender their role in the belief that the ones who proposed the idea were men. The demands and accomplishments of the women in *Ecclesiazusae* are actually what make the story comical. They are, according to Athenian democratic standards, illogical and silly. As Xenophon said, their intelligence was not measured by their level of worldly knowledge, but by their ability to obey men. Hence, classical Athenian reality would have deemed it unthinkable to consider women in positions of political leadership. They were not intellectually competent enough to do so. This might cause one to question the purpose of Aristophanes's play. More to the point, it forces one to wonder why he chose to portray Athenian democratic men as bumbling, gullible fools. They did, in the end, relinquish their role as assemblymen to the women. Herein lies the correlation between literature and reality that reveals the true role of women in ancient Athens. In *Ecclesiazusae*, Chremes speaks of one of the men at the assembly who demanded that women should run the country. Unaware that the man was actually a woman in disguise he says, "He maintained that women were both clever and thrifty, that they never divulged the Mysteries of Demeter, while you and I go about babbling incessantly about whatever happens at the Senate."[16]

In this passage, Aristophanes was not implying that women in the real world were more intelligent and therefore should run the country. Rather, an honorable Athenian woman remained indoors where she learned to be both clever and thrifty in managing the household. Wives were responsible for stocking fruits, grains, vegetables and raw wool for eventual utilization and consumption. Their efficiency and reliability left men free to take care of affairs in the field and at the assembly.[17] By placing women in the public sphere, Aristophanes exploited their socially and politically incompetent status to describe the state of his country at the hands of incompetent men. Thus, the above passage reads more like a veiled historiographical reference to the condition of the senate in the real world.

While, on first pass, Herodotus's accounts might seem as if he were trying to redeem a woman's position in society, most of the cunning females he wrote about were not even Athenian. For example, when Lydian king Candaules tried to prove to his chief adviser, Gyges, that his wife was the most beautiful, he paid the ultimate price. After discovering that her husband had arranged to have Gyges secretly view her while she undressed, she conspired with Gyges, to murder her husband, the king. At the appointed moment, Gyges killed the hapless king and seized both queen and kingdom for himself.[18] This account underscores how Athenian men ought not to behave. Under a monarchy, women, unrestrained by men, became more devious than Aristophanes's heroines, while kings acted more foolishly than the playwright's male characters. Athenian democracy expected women to be controlled by men and men to be more effective leaders than autocratic monarchs. The freedoms men enjoyed under a democracy allowed them to collectively make sound decisions that would strengthen their administration and maintain their liberty. To Herodotus, it made no sense not to exercise their civil liberties. The Athenians knew all too well the price they had to pay for not employing their intellect. Phye is the only woman to appear in an Athenian setting in Herodotus's *Histories*. Represented as a tall beauty, she was paraded about by the tyrant Peisistratus, dressed in such a way as to appear to be the goddess Athene herself. By not exercising sound judgment, the people instantly fell for Peisistratus's scam.[19] The result, of course, was that the Athenians were naïve enough to make him their leader and subsequently paid the price of tyrannical rule. Although much of Peisistratus's reign in the sixth century BC was relatively benign and successful, tyrants typically established their rule by unlawful force. Hence, the community did not benefit from the collective, intellectual decision-making process of a democratic assembly, which is what Herodotus highly valued.[20]

Herodotus and Religion

Identifying Herodotus's democratic interests in the *Histories* require close examination. They are not explicitly apparent, but they were no doubt inspired by the growing intellectual ferment of philosophical thought that was spreading in the Greek world in the fifth century BC. Yet it is also clear that Herodotus did not overtly express agnosticism, which in his lifetime might have carried a penalty of execution. It is necessary to keep in mind that the concept of freedom at this time was still relatively new. The canopy that protected freedom of ideas was still quite small and inequitable by today's standards. The freedom of religious expression may have been a part of its evolving process. Perhaps, to avoid trouble for spreading impious ideas, the presence of the gods in Herodotus's writings was still quite notable. Since we know little about his religious convictions, one can presume he safely moderated the growing belief that men were the authors of their own fate by attributing certain outcomes to divine forces.[21] Such was the story of Xerxes's and Artabanus's dreams regarding the invasion of Greece. Artabanus's psychological explanation of the dreams altered when he admitted to having been visited by the gods. As long as the moral of the story favored the role of the gods, Herodotus was safe. His readers, nonetheless, gained the benefit of considering the veiled pragmatic solutions to life as promoted by democracy.

Conclusion

By the time Herodotus wrote and published the *Histories* most of the events of which he spoke had already taken place. While he is not known to have had any military experience, it is important to keep in mind that military participation did not guarantee historical accuracy. For example, Greco-Roman historian Polybius, who had an active career in politics and even fought in the Achaean war, had forged a lifelong friendship with the Roman General Scipio Aemilianus during his sixteen-year detention in Rome. Because of this, one must consider the possibility of a hidden Roman agenda, which, in this case, was undoubtedly meant to dissuade Greek opposition to Rome.[22]

Since Herodotus is the first in an ancient line of historians to come out of Europe, the discipline of history, as shaped by him, was rudimentary insofar as research and methodology, which explains why his writings read more like a novel than a historical military account. Despite the difficulties related to the plausibility of ancient writing, Herodotus's accounts remain the most complete retelling of the Greco-Persian wars. It stands as a matter of personal discretion whether it is reasonable to assume that his accounts were not so much a record of military history as they were propaganda for democracy, modeled on that of Athens, and intended to benefit Greek culture as a whole.

Notes

1. Herodotus, "Histories" in *Herodotus, On the War for Greek Freedom: Selections from the Histories,* trans. Samuel Shirley, ed. James Romm (Indianapolis: Hackett Publishing, 2001), viii.

2. Everett L. Wheeler and Barry Strauss, "Battle," in *The Cambridge History of Greek and Roman Warfare,* eds. Philip Sabin, Hans van Wees, and Michael Whitby (Cambridge University Press, 2007), 190.

3. Richard A. Gabriel, "Can We Trust the Ancient Texts?" *Military History* 25.1 (2008): 63.

4. Herodotus, 121.

5. Sara Forsdyke, "Athenian Democratic Ideology and Herodotus' "Histories," *American Journal of Philology* 122.3 (2001): 334.

6. Herodotus, 122.

7. Forsdyke, 348.

8. Herodotus, xiii.

9. Ibid. 137.

10. Christopher W. Blackwell, "The Development of Athenian Democracy," in Adriaan Lanni, ed., "Athenian Law in its Democratic Context" (*Center for Hellenic Studies On-line Discussion*

Series). Republished in C.W. Blackwell, ed., *Dēmos: Classical Athenian Democracy* (A. Mahoney and R. Scaife, ed., *The Stoa: a consortium for electronic publication in the humanities* [www.stoa.org]) edition of January 24, 2003.: 3, accessed November 6, 2015. http://www.stoa.org/projects/demos/ article_democracy_development?page=3&greekEncoding=UnicodeC.

11. Herodotus, 11.

12. Ibid, 104.

13. Ibid, 94.

14. Ibid, xvi.

15. Xenophon, *Economics* 10.1; The Perseus Catalog, accessed, April 4, 2015, http:// www.perseus.tufts.edu/hopper/text?doc=Perseus%3Atext%3A1999.01.0212%3Atext%3DEc.% 3Achapter%3D7%3Asection%3D22.

16. Aristophanes, *Ecclesiazusae* 121; The Perseus Catalog, accessed, March 12, 2015, http://www.perseus.tufts.edu/hopper/text?doc=Perseus%3Atext%3A1999.01.0030%3Acard%3D41442 -444.

17. Sarah B. Pomeroy, Stanley M. Burstein, Walter Donlan, and Jennifer Tolbert Robert, *Ancient Greece: A Political, Social and Cultural History*, 3d ed. (Oxford: Oxford University Press, 2011), 265.

18. Herodotus, 6.

19. Emily Katz Anhalt, "Seeing is Believing: Four Women on Display in Herodotus' *Histories*," *New England Classical Journal* 35, no. 4 (2008): 271.

20. Blackwell, n.p. http://www.stoa.org/projects/demos/article_democracy_development? page=3&greekEncoding=UnicodeC.

21. Herodotus, xvii.

22. Wheeler, 191.

Bibliography

Aristophanes. *Ecclesiazusae* 121; The Perseus Catalog. Accessed, March 12, 2015,
    http://www.perseus.tufts.edu/hopper/text?doc=Perseus%3Atext%
    3A1999.01.0030%3Acard%3D41

Blackwell, Christopher W. "The Development of Athenian Democracy." in
    Adriaan Lanni, ed., "Athenian Law in its Democratic Context" (*Center for
    Hellenic Studies On-line Discussion Series*). Republished in C.W.
    Blackwell, ed., *Dēmos: Classical Athenian Democracy* (A. Mahoney and
    R. Scaife, edd., *The Stoa: a consortium for electronic publication in the
    humanities* [www.stoa.org]) edition of January 24, 2003. Accessed
    November 6, 2015. http://www.stoa.org/projects/demos/
    article_democracy_development?page=3&greekEncoding=UnicodeC.

Forsdyke, Sara, "Athenian Democratic Ideology and Herodotus' *Histories*,"
    American Journal of Philology 122.3 (2001): 329-358.

Gabriel, Richard A., "Can We Trust the Ancient Texts." *Military History* 25.1
    (2008): 62-70.

Hanson, Victor Davis. *Carnage and Culture.* New York: Anchor House Books, a
    Division of Random House Inc., 2001.

Herodotus, "Histories*"* in *On the War for Greek Freedom: Selections from the
    Histories.* Translated by Samuel Shirley. Edited by James Romm.
    Indianapolis: Hackett Publishing, 2001.

Pomeroy, Sarah B., Stanley M. Burstein, Walter Donlan, and Jennifer Tolbert
    Roberts.
    Ancient Greece: A Political, Social and Cultural History. 3d ed. Oxford:
    Oxford University Press, 2011.

Wheeler, Everett L. and Barry Strauss, "Battle," in *The Cambridge History of
    Greek and Roman Warfare.* Edited by Philip Sabin, Hans van Wees, and
    Michael Whitby. Cambridge University Press, 2007.

Xenophon. *Economics* 7.22; The Perseus Catalog. Accessed April 4, 2015. http://
    www.perseus.tufts.edu/hopper/text?doc=Perseus%3Atext%
    3A1999.01.0212%3Atext%3DEc.%3Achapter%3D7%3Asection%3D22

Kathryn Warner. *Edward II, The Unconventional King.* Stroud, UK: Amberley Publishing, 2014.

Book Review

Kathleen Guler

At first glance, the popular impression of King Edward II of England (1284-1327, r. 1307-1327) persists that he was a weak, immature, effeminate failure of a king who lusted after his male "favorites," was bullied by his powerful father Edward I Longshanks, and loathed by his long-suffering wife Isabella of France (1295-1358). Much material has been produced about Edward, but unfortunately, large amounts of it are twisted versions of reality, perpetuated rumors, or outright falsehoods. Fictionalized modern accounts, found in novels and movies such as *Braveheart*, further mislead readers' and viewers' preconceptions about Edward. Fortunately, historian Kathryn Warner has written an important biography of this king that exposes both his real quirks and the inaccuracies attached to him, all placed within the context of England's political position in fourteenth-century Europe.

Holding two degrees in medieval history from the University of Manchester, Warner is a well-respected expert on Edward II and the fourteenth century. Her study is based almost completely on primary sources, built on a daunting number of scraps of information found in documents ranging from letters and speeches in Edward's own words, letters from others surrounding him, itineraries, and various administrative rolls to royal household records, papal letters, and chamber journals. What emerges is not only a richly detailed account of the king's life, but a fascinating look at his personality that has been hidden behind innuendo and fabrications for centuries.

As the story of Edward's life unfolds, Warner focuses on the notorious controversies and myths that have grown up around him over time. One of the most persistent was his close bond with his male friends, in particular, Piers Gaveston (*c*.1284-1312) in the early part of the reign and Hugh Despenser the Younger (*c*.1286-1326) towards the end of it. Speculation and rumor have plagued writers' works on Edward from the earliest chroniclers to modern historians, suggesting that his closeness to these men meant he was either bisexual or homosexual. In her chapters on Piers Gaveston, who was the second of four sons of a poor Gascon knight and who had been a squire in Edward I's household and later a talented soldier in the army, Warner points out that his and Edward's rapport might have been misinterpreted through the ubiquitous usage of words such as "love." "The early fourteenth century was an age when men bandied about declarations of love for other men far more easily than in later eras" (p.29), meaning it had a different connotation at that time. Chroniclers of the day designated this closeness as "improper," but Warner also clearly points out these writers were unreliable sources that had strong biases against the king, reflecting the mood of England's nobility towards his relationship with Gaveston. The chroniclers likely were trying to gain the aristocracy's favor. The author also notes that Christopher Marlowe's play *Edward II*, written *c.* 1592, a purely fictional rendition, certainly perpetuated the preconceived notion, carrying it into modern times with each of its continued productions. While Warner concedes that from the surviving evidence no absolute proof can be determined whether Edward's relationships with his favorites were sexual, she notes that both Edward and Gaveston took wives, had children, and even fathered illegitimate children, all in the traditional sense, suggesting that they were simply close friends who chose to defy the growing angst of England's powerful nobles.

Edward's queen, Isabella of France (m. 1308), was supposedly long-suffering, ignored, and despised. Here again Warner carefully examines the surviving documentation and reveals strong clues that Edward and Isabella probably had a warm, even loving, marriage for many years. In one of her letters to him, she called him "my very sweet heart" five times, and he called her his "dear heart" (p.47). Whether—or how much—Isabella was exasperated at the presence of Piers Gaveston during the favorite's years around Edward is not known, but the impression is that she tolerated the situation, whatever it entailed.

How Isabella viewed Edward's relationship with his second predominant "favorite," Hugh Despenser the Younger, was quite another matter. Isabella detested him. Unlike the arrogant but apparently tolerable Gaveston, Despenser appears to have been coldly calculating and greedy, gradually gaining control over Edward's political and financial power. Close to the time that Despenser's "friendship" with Edward deepened, the king's marriage began to sour. Although Warner skirts around the possibility that the favorite caused a major rift between the royal couple, she hints that Despenser may have been a catalyst behind Isabella's departure for France in 1325, never to return to her husband. There, she eventually allied with the exiled nobleman Roger Mortimer, a sworn enemy of both Despenser and Edward. Rumors developed of an affair with Mortimer and whether her eldest child, the future Edward III (1312-1327), could have actually been Mortimer's son. Warner finds no evidence that Isabella and Mortimer were ever lovers. Instead, the author presents the strong likelihood that they were only political allies. Further, Isabella could not have met Mortimer until years *after* her last child was born in 1321. Warner also shows proof that Edward and Isabella were together when each of their four children was conceived. Interestingly, based on the period's events Isabella allegedly earned the nickname "She-Wolf of France" (p. 39). However, that epithet was actually Shakespeare's title for Margaret of Anjou, mistakenly applied to Isabella in 1757 by poet Thomas Grey.

Throughout the book, Warner highlights Edward's inadequacy as a king, the odd hobbies that made him the butt of jokes, and his generosity. On the one hand, Edward paid little attention to his country, neglecting important political issues while he spent time with his favorites. He also placed himself in the company of lowborn tradesmen, preferring their company and performing robust physical labor alongside them. He appears to have disliked any sort of regal and "idyllic" court life, which probably bored him. This caused a great amount of furor amongst his nobles, who disdained such work and considered it inappropriate for a king to enjoy. On the other hand, Edward was extremely generous to those around him—not only to his favorites, to Isabella, and to others of the aristocracy with whom he was pleased—but to strangers, messengers, and others on down the scale to the lowest ranks. While he was generous to a fault, unfortunately this strained his treasury, already depleted due to his father's wars. To give huge gifts of lands and titles to his favorites, especially the arrogant Gaveston and the hated Despenser, created serious animosity. Warner carefully examines the period when Edward's power waned: in September 1326, Isabella and Mortimer staged a small-scale but very successful invasion that resulted in Edward's deposition, Despenser's execution, and the placement of the young Edward III on the throne under Isabella and Mortimer's regency. Even while trying to avoid capture and after his imprisonment, Edward continued to show generosity; sometimes he is compared to the image of Nero fiddling away while Rome burned.

In the final chapter, "The Curious Case of the King Who Lived," Warner addresses the intriguing controversy of when and how Edward actually died. According to fourteenth century chroniclers, he supposedly died in late September 1327, murdered, first by suffocation, then "with a plumber's red-hot iron inserted through a horn leading to the inmost parts of the bowel, [his killers] burned out the respiratory organs beyond the intestines, taking care that no wound should be discernible on the royal body" (p. 243). This method of murder was handed down in numerous accounts over the years. Warner, however, refutes this as pure falsehood, first citing the unreliability of the chroniclers, and more importantly, laying out strong evidence that Edward may have survived for a few years past his alleged death date, perhaps up to 1330, or even later. While this evidence is not indisputable, it includes traces of at least four conspiracies to rescue Edward, the mysteries of why no one was allowed to view his body after his alleged death, why he was not buried for three months afterward, and why he was not laid in state like other kings. No details remain of his December 1327 funeral either. Most importantly, Warner cites letters that have surfaced which date to the years after the funeral, stating that Edward was "alive and in good health of body, in a safe place at his own wish [or command]" (p.248). Some conspirators of the time believed he was kept at Corfe Castle in Dorset, prompting armed plots to free him in 1329-1330. Other letters suggest Edward had fled to Italy and lived out his years there.

This biography includes a genealogy tracing from Edward's grandparents through four generations after him; a useful note on wages and prices of the period; several color plates, mostly of locations important to the biography plus photographs of related documents; and a warm foreword by historian Ian Mortimer, who gives the author a resounding endorsement. The one item missing is a map. Although most of the place names will be familiar to scholars of this period, a map showing their locations would have been a good addition.

Warner has pieced together a richly detailed puzzle that corrects many of the misconceptions about Edward II of England and produces a much more complete portrayal of his personality. Where the truth is unknown due to the lack of surviving evidence, Warner says so. Her approach is remarkably even-handed; while she points out the good things Edward did, she does not gloss over his terrible flaws. Warner's biography is a welcome addition to the collection of anyone studying this period. She will be following up with a biography of Isabella of France, due in spring 2016.

Eugene Rogan. *The Fall of the Ottomans: The Great War in the Middle East*. Basic Books: New York, 2015.

Book Review

Robert Smith, PhD.

Ironically, this review of Eugene Rogan's *The Fall of the Ottomans: The Great War in the Middle East* began on the same day that Omar Sharif—the actor most noted for his role in *Lawrence of Arabia*—died. That movie, along with T. E. Lawrence's *Pillars of Wisdom,* is often the sum of knowledge for many in the military, the government, and in academia about the fall of the Ottoman Empire. It is an unexplored dimension for many. Rogan's deft, insightful, and judicious handling of the political aspects of the empire's fall, coupled with a good overview of the related military campaigns, makes this a critical book to read and understand.

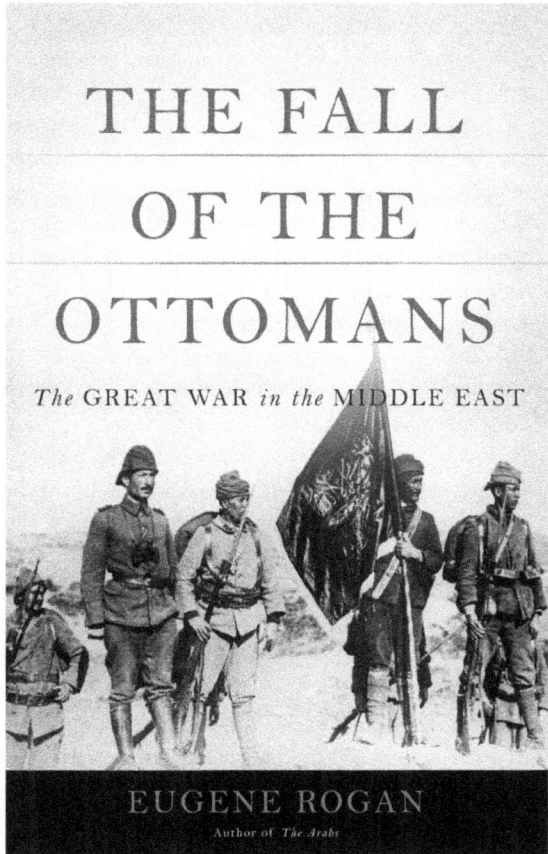

History—and Lawrence of Arabia—portray the Ottomans as bumblers. Granted, the previous several hundred years prior to World War One proved to be a series of reversals to the Ottoman Empire, following the defeat of their fleet to the Holy League of Europe at Lepanto in October 1571. Even more ruinous to the empire was the loss of its financial independence. When Ottomans became unable to meet their obligations to foreign creditors in the late nineteenth century, they were forced to make economic concessions to the Great Powers of Europe—Russia, Great Britain, France, Austria-Hungary, Italy, and Germany. In essence, the Ottomans abdicated control of the empire's finances to the Great Powers prior to World War One. In their quest for colonies and new markets known as the "Great Game," the European powers carved up slices of the Ottoman Empire from the Balkans to Libya. The Balkan Wars of Liberation were of even greater consequence to the empire's fall. These conflicts, fought on the eve of World War One, expelled the Ottomans from their centuries-old domains. In a sense, it is hard not to feel some empathy for an empire that did not know how to face the challenges that modernity and nationalism thrust upon it.

What really rivets the reader's attention is the Young Turk Movement's adoption of *Jihad* as both a wartime and social movement. In the past, most World War One historians paid this important and crucial aspect of Ottoman war-making scant attention. Several generations of historians have ignored this aspect of Ottoman strategy. It greatly concerned the British, however, as they struggled to hold onto India in wartime and to keep passions cooled between Moslems and Hindus. Germany was an enthusiastic advocate of the Ottomans' use of this card. Germany had no real Muslim population, so *jihad* was of no strategic internal consequence. For Austro-Hungary, however, it was another matter. Eventually, the British waged their own *jihad* against the subject peoples of the Ottoman Empire, leading—for example—to the birth of Saudi Arabia.

There will be many readers unhappy with how carefully Rogan seems to tread on the Armenian genocide controversy. In particular, Rogan does not reach any high and far-reaching moral condemnations. However, he does not shy away from the fact that the Ottomans massacred and destroyed the Armenians. Nor is he averse to using the G word—genocide. However, Rogan balances this with a storyline many may not know, and that is how the Armenian internal rebellions and aid given to Czarist Russia helped free themselves from the Ottomans. The evil is not lessened by that factor, but the explanation of why and how it happened becomes clearer.

The *Fall of the Ottomans* meets all this reviewer's tests of significance and enjoyment and his copy is VERY marked up with pencil for areas to use in university teaching, of interest, and for further research. It is difficult to keep from dashing through the book. It is excellent, and it requires the reader to force a leisurely pace to absorb all the new material. Rogan sets the A standard for those wanting to understand the Great War in the Middle East and its subsequent second, third, and fourth order effects today. The effects of the fall of the Ottoman Empire include the attacks of 9-11 and the rise of ISIS. Truly, this book calls out to all those interested in current world affairs.

Greg King and Penny Wilson. *Lusitania: Triumph, Tragedy, and the End of the Edwardian Age.* New York: St. Martins Press, 2015.

Book Review

Robinlynn Stewart

To commemorate the one-hundredth anniversary of the Lusitania tragedy, numerous historical narratives have sought to reexamine the events of May 7, 1915. Greg King and Penny Wilson's narrative, *Lusitania: Triumph, Tragedy, and the End of the Edwardian Age*, seeks to examine this tragedy through the perspective of its passengers and crew. King and Wilson, known for their collaborative works investigating the Russian royal family, provide a fascinating narrative, which examines the final days of the ship that nearly drove the United States into World War I.

Lusitania begins by addressing the circumstances surrounding the Cunard liner's fateful voyage in May 1915. King and Wilson assess the increasing sea threat posed by German U-boats cruising in British waters, as the Great War widened in scope and destructive capability throughout the first months of 1915. As established customs and courtesies of earlier European conflicts fell away and the British failed to abide by long-held carrier rules governing the conduct of ships at war, the German U-boat campaign became increasingly aggressive. On the date of Lusitania's departure from New York City, tensions between Great Britain and Germany in the war at sea had resulted in the German embassy's inclusion of a warning that any British or Allied ships, regardless of their cargo, would be at risk of attack.

This fear of attack resonated heavily with many of Lusitania's passengers as they boarded one of the fastest ships in the Cunard Line. Some were personally advised by the German embassy to forgo their passage on the Lusitania as its departure date neared. King and Wilson skillfully utilize the apprehension of Lusitania's passengers as they begin their biographies of those aboard. Their intense passenger biographies are excellently composed, and allow the narrative to keep readers engaged. The authors' ability to weave vivid and comprehensive biographies of their subjects allows a reader to forge a connection with these vibrant, yet flawed, passengers. Although King and Wilson's designation of Lusitania's passengers as a "Cast of Characters" trivializes their tragic experiences, it is more of an irritant than a deterrent to the overall narrative.

Wilson and King's character biographies include over sixty first- and second-class passengers, including: millionaire playboy Alfred Vanderbilt, acclaimed theater producer Charles Frohman, renowned actress Rita Jolivet, and American hotelier Albert Bilicke. King and Wilson attempt to utilize this extensive list of wealthy passengers to illustrate the excess and idealism of the Edwardian period as it clashes with the harsh realities of a world at war. In this endeavor, they are largely successful. Unfortunately, this extensive and detailed series of biographies overwhelms the narrative, drastically minimizing the political, diplomatic, and military factors, which result in Lusitania's demise. King and Wilson also fall short in adequately addressing the plight of those third-class passengers aboard ship. While the authors readily acknowledge this deficiency in their prologue, claiming a scarcity of adequate source material, it presents an unbalanced social history of events onboard the liner during that fateful cruise. To try to remedy this deficiency, the narrative utilizes several crew accounts to depict the common man's experience.

As Wilson and King weave together the numerous biographies of their subjects, they place them against the backdrop of one of the last storied luxury liners of the early twentieth century. Considered one of the fastest ships afloat in 1915, Lusitania was the preeminent liner of the period. Lusitania not only held the benefit of speed for the dangerous voyage across the Atlantic, it was outfitted with rich, tasteful architecture, suitable for transporting some of the Edwardian age's most notable passengers.

Against the backdrop of these Palladian lounges and richly outfitted smoking rooms, readers are introduced to Lusitania's captain, William Turner. King and Wilson develop their narrative's thesis around Captain Turner's conduct. The authors claim that the captain's ineffectiveness, duplicity, and negligence were the primary factors in the tragedy. To build this case, King and Wilson utilize several primary sources: witness accounts, logbooks, telegrams, and court testimony. They cite the captain's failure to stage lifeboat drills, his unfamiliarity with a new crew, and his apathy towards passenger inquiries regarding their safety as they entered the war zone. Turner's actions left those aboard Lusitania unprepared when disaster struck. Furthermore, first-hand accounts claim that Turner was duplicitous as he assured several first-class passengers the Lusitania would receive an armed escort as they entered the war zone, despite knowledge to the contrary. Others noted Turner's refusal to give the order to abandon ship, even as seawater rushed upon the decks of the debilitated vessel. King and Wilson go further in their assertion of Turner's culpability, as they describe the captain's decision to ignore telegrams warning ships of German U-boats lurking off the southern coast of Ireland on May 7, 1915. The Captain's most significant errors may have been his decision to ignore the zigzag maneuvers suggested by the British Admiralty to elude the enemy, his orders to slow the speed of Cunard's fastest liner, and his decision to steer the ship in waters expressly noted as being hazardous.

The narrative's strongest prose can be found in the chapters outlining Lusitania's final eighteen minutes. The authors' diligence in creating the lengthy biographical sketches of passengers is utilized during the disaster as these men, women, and children desperately struggled to survive. These gripping moments address the failures of the crew, as they refused to aide frantic passengers, were unable or unwilling to deploy lifeboats, took lifebelts from passengers, and—as one account alleges—a member of the crew even attacked a passenger with an ax during the chaos. King and Wilson provide a concise account of events as Lusitania sank beneath the waves and its survivors were forced to wait hours for rescue, although the coast was within their sight. As the survivors waited for rescue, *Lusitania: Triumph, Tragedy, and the End of the Edwardian Age* poignantly examines the final moments of those passengers who survived the sinking, but could not survive the frigid waters as they awaited rescue. The author's descriptions of rescue operations are grim, peppered with only the occasional happy ending, such as the tale of a missing child that was reunited with his family.

The narrative is fairly short for such a weighty subject, comprising only 299 pages of text. The writing style is straightforward and designed to address the casual reader. Although designed for a general audience, *Lusitania: Triumph, Tragedy, and the End of the Edwardian Age* provides a detailed notes and bibliography section, immensely useful to those academic historians seeking to further investigate this topic. While the text does attempt to address the implications the Lusitania disaster had for American isolationist sentiment and on the emergence of the preparedness movement, it still lacks the richness of military, diplomatic, and political analysis that readers may find in a strictly academic account. *Lusitania: Triumph, Tragedy, and the End of the Edwardian Age* is a great narrative for admirers of social history works featuring the upper classes of society; however, for more academic readers, the text may be more of a quick recreational read. In this respect, *Lusitania: Triumph, Tragedy, and the End of the Edwardian Age* should be considered for its smooth flow and excellent biographical content.

Michael Walzer. *Just and Unjust Wars: A Moral Argument with Historical Illustrations.* 5th ed. New York: Basic Books, 2015.

Book Review

Cynthia Nolan, PhD

The classic book on the subject of just war has been reissued. Michael Walzer's 1977 authoritative exploration of war, *Just and Unjust Wars: A Moral Argument with Historical Illustrations* is a staple in graduate schools across the country, and this fifth edition adds a new introduction on asymmetric warfare. Every edition of the book has kept the same body but added a new spin related to the wars in vogue at the time. The first book—Vietnam War. The second edition—Gulf War. The third edition—humanitarian intervention. The fourth edition—regime change. Now, almost fifty years after the first publication of this book, Walzer's arguments still stand as the most persuasive comments on just war ever published.

The heart of the Walzer argument is that moral concepts can be applied to war and have been throughout history. He illustrates just decisions through Ancient Greece, Ancient Rome, China, WWI, WWII, and more. He assures us that just war is an inherited code of conduct conforming to morality of which all men are aware. Throughout history, he sees comprehensive and consistent moral judgments applied to all wars. Indeed, man's understanding of morality is so common and sufficiently stable that shared judgments are possible, and that is what Walzer illustrates.

So, what is just war in this shared environment? For Walzer, it is a limited war, which has moral means and ends. It is conservative; it does not seek to usurp sovereignty, and it seeks the restoration of the status quo ante. *Jus in bello* applies to the conduct of war, and *jus ad bellum* applies to the decision to go to war. Throughout history, Walzer sees examples of each. On *jus in bello*, for instance, although outside observers might point to the My Lai incident as evidence that not everyone does conduct war justly, he points to it as an aberration; it was an extreme example of a routine policy gone wrong. Rather than pointing to the atrocities themselves, Walzer emphasizes the reaction to it. It was very clearly and widely acknowledged as an example of unjust conduct. He cites universal prohibitions against torture, slavery, and murder.

On *jus ad bellum*, he says that war is sometimes justified. For example, he argued that intervention should look as much like non-intervention as possible. The preventative war of balance is not just for Walzer. However, a counter intervention to restore the status quo is just. Indeed, the American intervention in Vietnam was not justified according to Walzer, and he has explored other decisions in his 2004 book of collected essays: *Arguing War*. This 2004 book is, in some ways, easier to read than *Just and Unjust Wars*. The 1977 book spends a lot of time on the theory, while the 2004 book can focus on contemporary specifics.

Just war is, of course, not the only way to describe wartime decisions (either within war or prior to war). Walzer grapples with the realist notion of self-interest and survival by illustrating the strong historical trend of justice. Men do not conduct war—and never have—as if "might equals right" or "all is fair in war." It is a practical morality, for Walzer. Indeed, morality can only refer to what occurs in the real world, not to general theories of right and wrong. Moral knowledge and principles do not change over time, and we are subject to common moral constraints as illustrated in Walzer's examples.

The book can get a bit tedious as Walzer covers centuries of philosophy and theory, but this is the ONE book on just war to which everyone who writes on this subject must refer. If you are at all interested in the subject, you must start here even if Walzer's argument can get a bit complicated. This is a history of just war, and it owes all of its arguments to the historical illustrations that Walzer chooses. You might choose different examples, and/or you might want to ask for a specific list of how to apply just war. Walzer does not give a simple list, however.

Traditional just war theory has some long-established rules coming from Catholic theologians of the third century and beyond. These rules are built on proper authority, just cause, and right intention. For a simple description, one need only consult the Catechism of the Catholic Church (CCC 2302-2317) in which a just war fulfills four criteria: 1. War is a response to lasting, grave, and certain damage; 2. All other means of solving the problem are exhausted; 3. There is a serious prospect of success; 4. War does not produce evil graver than the evil to be eliminated. Walzer does not simplify his descriptions into four points like this, and his arguments are always rooted in the rather lengthy and extensive moral vocabulary of shared judgments.

Walzer acknowledges his debt to Catholic theologians, but he refuses to adopt their structure of right and wrong. Walzer's just war is not about religion, the Commandments, or love for humanity. His just war is valid because history has made it so. War is a social creation, and we can judge it by its social or moral merits. As such, war has always had a code of conduct in which justice plays a very strong role, no matter what other observers might say.

Jared Diamond. *Guns, Germs, and Steel: The Fates of Human Societies*. New York: W.W. Norton & Company, Inc., 1999

Book Review

Will Hamblet

Most historians typically discuss history by focusing on certain events or points in time. That one event or era is typically large enough for historians to dissect for months or even years to become experts on that specific period. Researching large amounts of time is a daunting task, and most historians would consider the thought of covering over 13,000 years of history in one book to be absurd. However, Jared Diamond dared to tackle that endeavor by examining why different cultures followed different courses in history.

Diamond attempted to answer the question of why Europeans conquered the majority of the world. A friend of his from New Guinea, Yali, inspired him when he asked Diamond this question: "Why is it that you white people developed so much cargo and brought it to New Guinea, but we black people had little cargo of our own?" (p. 14). While most anthropologists would be quick to point out racial differences, Diamond focused on environmental differences surrounding cultures. He tackled Yali's question in a four-part answer by discussing the rise of civilizations, the rise and spread of food production, germ exchange through cultural collisions, and why some cultures remained hunter-gatherers while others became food producers. The four parts of the book deliver an interesting take on 13,000 years of history while providing an unbiased assessment of why Europeans subjugated much of the world.

While Diamond did a wonderful job providing an explanation of these four parts in an attempt to answer Yali's question, his discussion only touched the tip of historical discussion through a scientific approach. He explored "chains of causation" in a scientific manner and described why some cultures dominated the world; however, the book failed to provide the details necessary to be a true history book. Nevertheless, Diamond noted that he intended this book to convince the reader that "history is just not one damned fact after another" (p. 31). While it does succeed in providing a great explanation of cultural differences through an analytical or scientific lens, historical facts have their place—especially when discussing a specific event and why things happened.

Diamond provided wonderful insight into why some cultures dominated others by constantly referring back to factors of science such as the domestication of animals, exposure to germs, and farm production. However, he failed to address the most controversial wild card of history—human thought and ingenuity, and discounted more than 13,000 years of human ingenuity for scientific factors. The ingenuity and thought of humans played a significant role in history throughout those years. Humans created the social, political, and military framework, which affected the scientific factors that Diamond discussed in his book. History identifies the peculiar, and addresses the architecture behind political, legal, social, and religious infrastructure. Human thought and ingenuity play a large role in all of this, and discounting this wild card creates a vast flaw within the book's theory that random chance dealt Europeans all the cards of scientific factors. However, Diamond should be praised for his attempt to bridge disciplinary fields to shed light on thousands of years of history. This book helps to provide students of history with wonderful context that there are also scientific factors that play a part in history.

John France. *Western* Warfare in the Age of the Crusades, 1000-1300. Ithaca, New York: Cornell University Press, 1999.

Book Review

Geoffrey Fisher

Professor John France of Swansea University owns a lofty reputation in medieval military history circles. His book, *Western Warfare in the Age of the Crusades, 1000-1300*, is an attempt to shed light on the socio-economic characteristics of medieval warfare. France's book presents three fascinating arguments.

First, his discussion about how medieval Europe fought its wars encapsulates how warfare at this time consisted of haphazard engagements. European medieval society was comprised of decentralized governmental systems. France calls the spheres of power in European society the *mouvances*. These consisted of well-heeled medieval families. For example, the Counts of Anjou ruled from Western France, the Baldwins ruled in Jerusalem, the Dukes of Brabant ruled from the south of the Netherlands, and the royal houses of Hohenstaufen and Capetians ruled from Germany and France, respectively. All of this economic, military, and political dispersion made it difficult for any one family to maintain a lasting hold on the European continent. If the political and military leaders wanted to fight wars, then they had to conduct it through indirect means, namely raiding, pillaging, and ambushing one's opponents. This indirect way of war made a lot of sense since limited logistical abilities of the state restricted large-scale warfare. In addition, a direct conflict jeopardized the nobilities' position of power should the outcome be negative.

The second argument France discusses is the primacy of the castle. He dedicated two chapters to castles and fortifications and how they impacted wars and sieges. The primacy of the castle can be found in its construction. Castles protected the inhabitants from both domestic and foreign threats. For instance, the castle's walls assisted in helping to protect governments from rebellion by the native populace as well as external coercion.[1] The castle's defensively strong characteristics often held the advantage in battle and medieval governmental infrastructure helped to maintain the castle's prominent role in European society. France writes that castles held "a military purpose—to defend the life and goods of its owner and to provide his troops with a base."[2] The number of castles increased throughout the Middle Ages and reinforced this basic component of war.[3] One of the benefits of the castle in a war was that it protected the troops from enduring enemy attacks. For example, after ransacking the surrounding landscape the enemy grew tired. Protected from the initial attack, the rested garrisoned troops inside the castle sallied out and laid waste to weakened opponents. During the medieval period, conducting a siege against a garrisoned castle often led to a long and protracted expedition. If a ravaging army decided to besiege an enemy's castle, they left themselves vulnerable to attack from relief forces. This created a situation where those conducting the siege found themselves surrounded by the besieged and their allies.

The third argument comes at the end of his book where France recognizes a paradox in medieval society. It was highly militarized, but at the same time, it lacked war academies. France is correct to point out that a lack of instruction in war solidified the power of the nobility. When medieval armies did go to war, their political and military leaders sought out conservative objectives. These leaders knew that their armies did not have the resources to conduct an extended war.

His list of sources is impressive. The historiography represented draws from a list of well-known medieval military historians. Bernard S. Bachrach, Kelly Devries, Stephan Morillo, Helen Nicholson, and Michael Prestwich are a few of his secondary sources.

Although this book has an illuminating thesis and fascinating historical arguments, one is bound to find a few criticisms. First, the reader may find that France's book lacks a prologue and an epilogue to introduce and conclude with his main thoughts to the reader. Second, he refers to many battles without equipping the reader with an adequate supply of maps. The great number of battles and sieges France lists makes it easy to get lost in the text. If he had focused only on the most consequential engagements, readers might not get easily lost. Third, the content is advanced and this creates confusion for newcomers to the discipline. For instance, it is easy for the newcomer to get lost when France is discussing the Maciejowski Bible and stone machicolations and how they relate to his central thesis. Diagrams of machicolations in use can be helpful to the reader. For the above reasons the work is in need of revision.

In closing, John France's book deftly blends the *mouvances* in European society. The socio-economic infrastructure of European culture led to the inability of military and political leaders to execute a plan that resulted in a decisive conflict. Even though the medieval world might seem distant in our technological society, the study of warfare during the Middle Ages is the study of hegemonies vying for control over the continent. European culture needs to acknowledge that "hegemonic" warfare is a historical legacy of Western identity.[4] Any student who is specializing in medieval warfare would do well to place France's book on their bookshelf.

Notes

1. John France, *Western Warfare in the Age of the Crusades, 1000-1300* (Ithaca, New York: Cornell University Press, 1999), 83.

2. Ibid., 84.

3. Ibid.

4. Garret Fagan and Matthew Trundle, eds., *New Perspectives on Ancient Warfare: History of Warfare* (Leiden: Brill, 2010), 215, accessed November 1, 2015, https://books.google.com.

Mirjam Pressler. *Treasures From the Attic: The Extraordinary Story of Anne Frank's Family*. New York: Doubleday, 2011

Book Review

Jennifer Thompson

Many people around the world have read *The Diary of Anne Frank*. Few have investigated to learn more about other members of her family. Helene Elias, Anne's aunt and sister of Anne's father Otto, inherited their mother's home, which included over six thousand documents of photos, letters, drawings, poems, and postcards. When Elias died, Buddy (Anne's cousin and childhood playmate) inherited this "treasure trove of historic importance" (inside book cover). Anne's family had written many times to one another before, during, and after the war. Buddy's wife, Gertrude (Gerti), and Mirjam Pressler (who translated Anne's diary into German) have used these documents to tell this extraordinary account of the story of Anne's family. Readers will learn about members of Anne's family, where they were during the war, the impact of the war on their lives, and how they survived after the war.

Readers first meet Anne's grandmother, Alice (Stern) Frank and see her childhood portrait, painted by Frankfurt Professor Schlesinger. This does not bring fond memories for her, as he would sternly reprimand her for any movement. "She knew she would have to stand still, not move her feet even if her legs became stiff and started to hurt, not turn her head to look at a fly, that it was just as forbidden to scratch anywhere if it itched" (p. 14). She could not refuse to go because her governess constantly reminded her that her father had spent a lot of money for the portrait. This painting hung in her parents' home until her father's death, in her mother's room at her grandfather's until her death, and then in her homes in Frankfurt and then in Basel, Switzerland. In 1935, she decided to write her life story to give to her three sons and one daughter on her seventieth birthday. "Alice had the good fortune to be born into a family where many stories were told and much was handed down from one generation to the next" (p. 39). As a young man, her grandfather, Elkan Cahn, had lived in the ghetto in *Judengasse* "Jews' Alley" in Frankfurt. The city council had forced the Jews to move there in 1462. Alice shared how she met Michael Frank. Her mother was against his becoming a son-in-law until Alice convinced her that "she had firmly decided to marry Michael and no one else" (p. 57). They married in 1886. They were not rich, but lived a better life than many. "The Franks were among the first in Frankfurt to get a telephone," and they "traveled often" (pp. 66, 67). Readers soon meet the children: Robert, Otto, Herbert, and finally daughter Helene (Leni). They moved several times and finally bought a large house at Jordanstrasse 4. Education, music lessons, and writing were important. The family also enjoyed parties, concerts, and plays. Michael's sudden death at the age of fifty-seven in 1909 was devastating to Alice. "It was her children that gave Alice the strength and courage to bear the difficult years that lay ahead—the years without Michael, as a widow" (p. 90). Alice inherited and now supervised the successful Michael Frank Bank, which suffered setbacks only because of WWI and the New York stock market crash in 1929.

Readers see the bonds between Otto and his family as they grew up and moved away from one another. The book documented many events in their lives with letters, poems, and newspaper articles. After his father's death, Otto "all but took over the father's role for his little sister" (p. 92). All three sons served in the military during World War I. Otto was working at the family bank and was the last one to marry when he married Edith Hollander on his birthday, May 12, 1925. Otto, Edith, Leni, and her husband Erich all lived in the family home with Alice, until after the birth of Margot. Otto and his family moved into a duplex in 1927, where Anne was born in 1929. The families were close, and the children visited Alice often. Erich accepted a job in Basel, Switzerland in 1929. The Frank Bank suffered another setback in 1931 with the arrest of Herbert for tax evasion. "He was accused of breaking the new regulations on securities trading with foreigners" (p. 122). He moved to Paris after his release and was not present for the hearing that pronounced him innocent. Leni and their two sons joined Erich in Basel, Switzerland in 1931. The Franks moved to a smaller apartment in 1931 and eventually back into the family home in 1932. After Hitler became Chancellor of the German Reich in 1933, the families decided to leave Germany. Alice moved to an apartment in Basel to be near Leni in 1933; Otto and his family moved to the Netherlands in 1934. Alice felt like an exile in Basel, but she enjoyed getting letters from her grandchildren, Margot and Anne. In 1938, Erich rented a big home so he could move his mother Ida to Basel. Alice moved in with them as well. News of events in Germany made the family glad they were safe from the Nazis. Alice was able to visit Otto's family in Amsterdam but fell ill and took awhile to recover. Edith's family left Germany during this time. "Edith's two brothers escaped to America and her mother came to join the Franks in Amsterdam" (p. 138). The Nazis invaded the Netherlands in 1940, and things became more difficult for Jews. Otto tried to get a visa for his family to go to

Cuba, the only way they could eventually reach America (since no visas were available to America in the Netherlands). "On December 1, 1941, Cuba actually did issue a visa for Otto Frank, but it was canceled as early as December 11" (p. 151). The family would now need to go into hiding. Leni received a mysterious birthday card from Otto's family in late July (her birthday was in September). "We can't correspond with . . . you all anymore" (p. 158). Jews in Switzerland soon learned they were no longer German citizens and must now surrender their passports. Switzerland denied many applications for citizenship from Jewish applicants.

The family in Basel started receiving news about the family. In March 1941, they learned that Leni's cousin, Jean-Michel, committed suicide in New York. They did not receive any news in 1942 and finally learned that England sent German Jews, including Robert, to a prison on the Isle of Man, where he remained for several months. A business letter from Otto's friend who had adult children hinted that Anne had grown taller. Erich's brother, Paul had a visa to go to Bolivia but could not go there from France or Switzerland. Herbert joined them in Switzerland using false papers using Jean-Michel's name. Leni's "flea market" became a real store in 1943, where emigrants sold belongings to raise money or to get rid of things they could not take with them. She held tea parties on Sundays and guests shared news of relatives still in danger.

When the war ended in 1945, Herbert returned to Paris. The family learned that Robert and his wife were safe in England. They received a telegram from Otto, who was heading to Paris. Four weeks later, they received a letter from Otto, who revealed their imprisonment in Auschwitz, the death of Edith, and his current search for Margot and Anne. More letters explain about their place of hiding, their capture, and ultimately the fate of the children. "The finality of the news left them nothing but helplessness and despair, especially Alice, who fell apart" (p. 226). Otto began to discuss Anne's diary. "I can't let the diaries out of my hands, there is too much in them that is not intended for anyone else, but I'll make excerpts" (p. 243). Friends convinced him that he should publish the diary. Alice finally saw Otto again on her eightieth birthday; he stayed for three weeks. Buddy became an actor and soon went on tour. He and Alice questioned whether Otto should publish Anne's private diary, but Otto felt "that she had an intellectual maturity that most adults don't have and maybe never will have" (p. 283). The family decided to buy the home in Basel, and Alice's health started to decline. Publishers released Anne's diary in Germany and France in 1950 and in England and the United States in 1952. In 1952, Erich and Leni finally became Swiss citizens, and Otto married Fritzi Geiringer and moved to the family home in Basel.

Buddy finally read the diary "and was deeply moved, shaken" and now understood "why Otto had said that he had never really known his daughter; Buddy felt the same way" (p. 302). Alice died a few months after her eighty-seventh birthday in 1953. "All four children of Michael and Alice Frank—Robert, Otto, Herbert, Leni—were together once more for their mother's funeral. It was to be the last time" (p. 317). Robert died two months later. After Anne's story came out in a play in 1955 and a movie in 1959, the diary became a worldwide bestseller. Otto established several foundations—Anne Frank Foundation in Amsterdam and the Anne Frank-Fonds in Basel—to manage the income from the diary "to contribute to better understanding between different religions, serve the cause of peace between peoples, and promote international contact between young people" (p. 362). Otto died in 1980. Erich died in 1984, and Leni died on the same day two years later.

"Anne Frank's diary had touched people, had gotten them to stop and reflect on their own memories of the catastrophe . . . awakened questions of guilt and responsibility . . . really changed people's lives. Its effects remain visible to this day" (p. 333). Buddy assumed the role to keep Anne's memory alive. His wife Gerti discovered the treasure trove of letters, photographs, and other documents in the attic of the family home. The Anne Frank-Fonds hired historian Dr. Peter Toebak to organize and archive all the material before moving them to the Anne Frank Foundation's archive in Amsterdam, "where every page was digitized or microfilmed" (p. 398). The Anne Frank-Fonds asked Gerti to take charge of creating a book from the letters and documents. They hired Mirjam Pressler to write this excellent book, which belongs on every bookshelf to gain a better understanding of Anne and her family.

William C. Davis. *Crucible of Command: Ulysses S. Grant and Robert E. Lee—The War The Fought, The Peace They Forged.* Da Capo Press: New York, 2015.

Book Review

Robert Smith, PhD.

It is easy to be glib about icons because with so much information out there already established, many seldom dig deeper. However much of what passes for assumed knowledge is not that. William C. Davis's new work, *Crucible of Command: Ulysses S. Grant and Robert E. Lee—The War They Fought, the Peace They Forged* will surprise even the most ardent Grant and Lee fans. The popular view is that these two American military legends are polar opposites. Yet a cursory examination will show they have much more in common than most credit. Both graduated from West Point. Both were outstanding horsemen, though Grant was superior. Both had hard economic times—including Grant's hardscrabble life and working as a clerk, but Lee's family finances from his father onward were fluid. Both fought in the Mexican-American War, and though Lee distinguished himself more, Grant was cited for coolness and bravery under fire. The real difference that runs implicit through Davis's book is where they came from and how it shaped and defined them. Lee was from an old "monied" and titled Tidewater family that even though they had fallen on hard times had lineage. Grant in contrast represented the new, muscular American West, where a man could rise above his family's station in life.

JFC Fuller's original study of these two men is exemplary. Fuller's work is perhaps the greater of the two works in pure military terms, yet Fuller missed points by not understanding the American character. Fuller theoretically understood Grant the general who became the Total War advocate—but not fully. What sets Davis's effort apart is that Davis understands the underpinning of the unique American experience that forged these men. Davis provides a truly comparative biography. Grant—the ever optimistic pragmatic thinker who looked for solutions, is summed up in this quote, "Stop worrying what Bobby Lee is going to do to you and start making him worry what *you* are going to do to *him!*" If something does not work, try again in a different fashion. Lee was cooler, perhaps more melancholy. The most telling aspect is Grant—Grant had friends—and his subordinates would call him "Sam." Never once did it seem that Lee had friends. There was simply a gap, be it social or something else, between Lee and everyone else. Yet Lee inspired and served as the glue that held the Army of Northern Virginia together through its slow offensive decline and starvation. One of the aspects that will prove surprising to almost any reader is the knowledge that Lee had a volatile temper. Those soldiers fought less for the Confederate States of America, than the family and the patriarch, Robert E. Lee. However, even this is tempered as Davis shows that Lee, though revered, was perhaps unloved by his staff. The use of snippets from Grant's letters show a degree of warmth that is missing from Lee's writings.

Davis brings a lot to this work. He is the author of many books on the American Civil War, as well as the retired Virginia Tech Director of Programs for the Virginia Center for Civil War Studies. The book is so well written it is easy to forget its deep roots in good scholarship and superb analysis. Despite its size and scholarship, it is a deceptively and surprisingly quick read. If a reader were to select only one book on these two men, this is the one. Works of this nature can grind into a tedious affair, but Davis's light hand keeps readers entertained—and learning—through the entire book.

Featured Titles from Westphalia Press

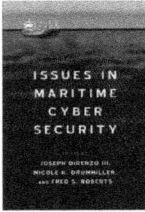

Issues in Maritime Cyber Security Edited by Nicole K. Drumhiller, Fred S. Roberts, Joseph DiRenzo III and Fred S. Roberts

While there is literature about the maritime transportation system, and about cyber security, to date there is very little literature on this converging area. This pioneering book is beneficial to a variety of audiences looking at risk analysis, national security, cyber threats, or maritime policy.

The Death Penalty in the Caribbean: Perspectives from the Police Edited by Wendell C. Wallace PhD

Two controversial topics, policing and the death penalty, are skillfully interwoven into one book in order to respond to this lacuna in the region. The book carries you through a disparate range of emotions, thoughts, frustrations, successes and views as espoused by police leaders throughout the Caribbean

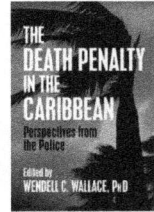

Middle East Reviews: Second Edition
Edited by Mohammed M. Aman PhD and Mary Jo Aman MLIS

The book brings together reviews of books published on the Middle East and North Africa. It is a valuable addition to Middle East literature, and will provide an informative read for experts and non-experts on the MENA countries.

Unworkable Conservatism: Small Government, Freemarkets, and Impracticality by Max J. Skidmore

Unworkable Conservatism looks at what passes these days for "conservative" principles—small government, low taxes, minimal regulation—and demonstrates that they are not feasible under modern conditions.

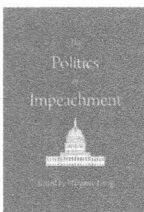

The Politics of Impeachment
Edited by Margaret Tseng

This edited volume addresses the increased political nature of impeachment. It is meant to be a wide overview of impeachment on the federal and state level, including: the politics of bringing impeachment articles forward, the politicized impeachment proceedings, the political nature of how one conducts oneself during the proceedings and the political fallout afterwards.

Demand the Impossible: Essays in History as Activism
Edited by Nathan Wuertenberg and William Horne

Demand the Impossible asks scholars what they can do to help solve present-day crises. The twelve essays in this volume draw inspiration from present-day activists. They examine the role of history in shaping ongoing debates over monuments, racism, clean energy, health care, poverty, and the Democratic Party.

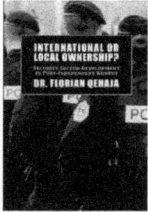

International or Local Ownership?: Security Sector
Development in Post-Independent Kosovo
by Dr. Florian Qehaja

International or Local Ownership? contributes to the debate on the concept of local ownership in post-conflict settings, and discussions on international relations, peacebuilding, security and development studies.

Donald J. Trump's Presidency: International Perspectives
Edited by John Dixon and Max J. Skidmore

President Donald J. Trump's foreign policy rhetoric and actions become more understandable by reference to his personality traits, his worldview, and his view of the world. As such, his foreign policy emphasis was on American isolationism and economic nationalism.

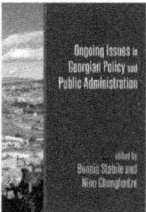

Ongoing Issues in Georgian Policy and Public Administration
Edited by Bonnie Stabile and Nino Ghonghadze

Thriving democracy and representative government depend upon a well functioning civil service, rich civic life and economic success. Georgia has been considered a top performer among countries in South Eastern Europe seeking to establish themselves in the post-Soviet era.

Poverty in America: Urban and Rural Inequality and
Deprivation in the 21st Century
Edited by Max J. Skidmore

Poverty in America too often goes unnoticed, and disregarded. This perhaps results from America's general level of prosperity along with a fairly widespread notion that conditions inevitably are better in the USA than elsewhere. Political rhetoric frequently enforces such an erroneous notion.

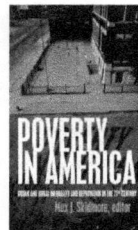

westphaliapress.org

www.ingramcontent.com/pod-product-compliance
Lightning Source LLC
Chambersburg PA
CBHW021930040426
42448CB00008B/992